The

MODERN WITCHCRAFT

SPELL BOOK

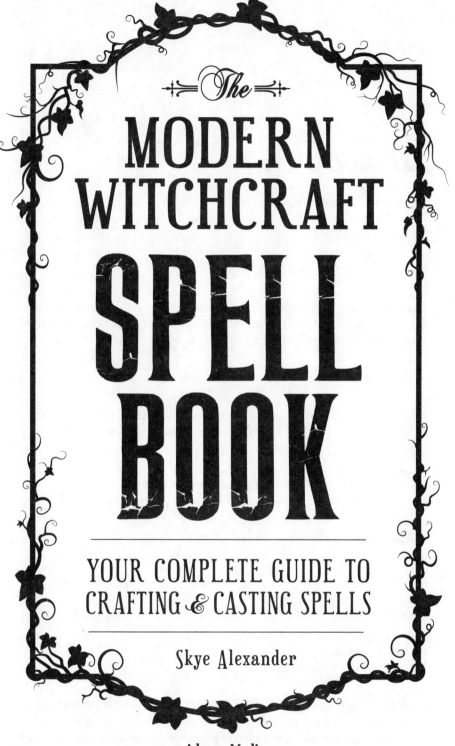

The

MODERN WITCHCRAFT

SPELL BOOK

YOUR COMPLETE GUIDE TO CRAFTING & CASTING SPELLS

Skye Alexander

Adams Media
New York   London   Toronto   Sydney   New Delhi

Adams Media
An Imprint of Simon & Schuster, Inc.
100 Technology Center Drive
Stoughton, MA 02072

For information about special discounts for bulk purchases, please contact Simon & Schuster Special Sales at 1-866-506-1949 or business@simonandschuster.com.

The Simon & Schuster Speakers Bureau can bring authors to your live event. For more information or to book an event contact the Simon & Schuster Speakers Bureau at 1-866-248-3049 or visit our website at www.simonspeakers.com.

Manufactured in the United States of America

14 2021

Library of Congress Cataloging-in-Publication Data has been applied for.

ISBN 978-1-4405-8923-2
ISBN 978-1-4405-8924-9 (ebook)

In memory of my mother, Joan Britton

Acknowledgments

Once again, I am indebted to my editors Tom Hardej and Peter Archer and all the amazingly talented folks at Adams Media for making this book possible.

CONTENTS

Introduction

SO YOU WANT TO BE A SPELLCASTER

Many of us were introduced to magick spells at an early age, through fairy tales, books, and movies. We saw Cinderella's fairy godmother transform a pumpkin into a jeweled coach drawn by a team of prancing horses. We witnessed a princess kiss a frog and turn him into a handsome prince. We watched Hermione Granger move trees with her magick wand. And we wanted to be able to wield that awe-inspiring power, too.

The good news is, you *do* have that power. Everyone has magickal ability—it's your birthright. And you know what else? You've probably already done lots of spells, but you just didn't realize it at the time. Blowing out candles on a birthday cake, for instance, is a popular good luck spell. Hanging an evergreen wreath on your front door is an ancient protection spell. Cursing a driver who steals your parking space, well, that's also a spell.

Simply put, a magick spell uses thoughts, words, and actions to cause certain changes to occur—and to generate outcomes through means that logic and conventional science can't explain. Have you ever made a wish that came true? That's magick at work. Would you like to be able to do that more often? You can. By training your mind and developing some natural skills that you already possess—and by aligning yourself with nature and the universe—you can create the reality you desire.

WHAT CONSTITUTES A SPELL?

Hollywood tends to focus on the sensational aspects of magick, witchcraft, and spellcasting, which can make the whole idea seem scary or weird or even ridiculous to many people. In reality, most witches and wizards don't put hexes on people; they don't turn frogs into princes or fly through the air on broomsticks; they don't brew eye of newt and tongue of dog in cauldrons for enchanted potions (although cauldrons still serve as handy tools in spellwork). Instead, modern-day magickal workers cast spells to help them get better jobs, attract love and friendship, safeguard their homes and families, and improve their health. You can even do a spell to find a parking space in a crowded shopping mall on the day after Thanksgiving.

According to Aleister Crowley, often recognized as the most powerful magician of the twentieth century, "Every intentional act is a magickal act." The purpose of a spell is to manifest something that you need or desire. That need or desire (or both) comprises your intent. When you cast a spell, your intent is vital to your success. Your *intention*, coupled with your *attention*, are the most important components in any spell—they're what make your wishes come true. That's why you'll often hear it said that magick is all in the mind. Beyond that, a spell might involve carefully orchestrated steps and procedures, exotic ingredients, cool clothes, and specialized equipment—all designed to increase the potency of the spell. It may also draw upon the forces of nature and/or supernatural powers.

WHAT YOU'LL LEARN FROM THIS BOOK

Few of us get the opportunity to attend Hogwarts for a magickal education. However, if you follow the guidelines in this book, you'll soon learn to cast spells for all sorts of purposes. You'll develop techniques for honing your mental and psychic powers. You'll find out how to tap the natural energies in plants and gemstones, and use them to augment your spells. You'll discover how to call upon spirits, deities, and other invisible beings to enhance your spellworking ability. Finally, you'll learn the best times to perform spells and rituals in order to produce the results you seek, safely and effectively.

Maybe you're not sure about all this stuff yet, but you're curious. Maybe you've dabbled with magick a bit and want to become more familiar with it. Maybe you're ready to take charge of your own destiny and start consciously creating the circumstances you desire in your life. If so, this book is for you.

PART I

Spellworking BASICS

Chapter 1

THE ART OF SPELLWORK

Magick is the art of creating change in accordance with your will. It's also what happens when you manipulate energy to produce a result, using methods that conventional science can't explain. Witches, wizards, shamans, and others who work with the magickal forces of the universe sometimes add the letter "K" to the word *magic* to distinguish it from stage illusion, card tricks, and the like.

Many people think that magick, witchcraft, and the process of casting spells are weird—maybe even a little spooky or evil. Unfortunately, for centuries suspicion, skepticism, confusion, and fear have muddied the magickal waters and interfered with the widespread use of spells to attract health, wealth, happiness, and all the other good things in life. The truth is, nothing is more natural than doing a spell. A long tradition of spellworking exists in most cultures, including Western culture. People from all walks of life have engaged in magick and spellworking for millennia, for myriad purposes. Today, curiosity about the art of spellcasting is growing rapidly—and as we gain more knowledge and become more familiar with magickal practices, the scary factor diminishes.

You've probably already cast spells without knowing it. For instance, wearing a ring set with your birthstone is an ancient good luck spell. Maybe you've wished upon a star or made a wish before blowing out candles on a birthday cake. In essence, wishing for something really, really hard is a kind of spell. If you want something badly enough, and you think about it constantly, you send out energy to attract that new reality you seek and help it come into being.

Daydreams aren't spells, however. The difference boils down to what spellcasters call intent. Intent means determining your objective and then performing an action with awareness, consciously channeling energy and emotion into the action in order to produce a result. Throughout this book, we'll talk about intent, focusing energy, creating images, and fueling your spells with emotion and willpower, for these are the keys to doing successful magick.

Avoid Obsession

Obsessing over a desire or need can actually prevent you from getting what you want. If you keep desperately hoping that your wish will come true, you exhibit doubt. And doubt squelches a spell's success like water poured on a fire.

WHAT, EXACTLY, IS A SPELL?

Simply put, a spell is something you do with clarity, intent, and awareness to generate a result. A spell consists of a set of thoughts and symbolic actions performed in the physical world to initiate change on a higher level. Once a change takes place at that higher level, it filters down and materializes here on earth. When you do a spell, you alter a situation by introducing new energy or rearranging the energy that's already present.

When doing a spell, you are the agent of change. You draw upon your own resources to gather and direct energy. You make it happen, and you take responsibility for your actions and their results. You may request assistance from a higher power to accomplish your objective, if you wish. Or you may bring in the energies of various substances, such as plants and gemstones, to augment your own powers. Ultimately, though, you're the writer, director, and producer.

WHY USE SPELLS?

People perform spells for a variety of reasons. Crafting and casting a spell allows you to take control of a situation—you no longer have to sit and wait for life to sort itself out. Spellwork is an active method of dealing with life, instead of passively accepting what comes your way. Engaging in spellwork can boost your confidence—there's nothing quite like seeing one of your spells materialize. Your self-esteem ratchets up a few notches, and you realize that you possess power you never knew you had before. However, if you just do spells to impress your friends or make yourself seem more important, you're missing out on magick's greater value.

Spellcraft also exercises your creativity. You might not be able to play the saxophone or paint a masterpiece or win a flamenco dance competition, but you can craft a web of energy from a variety of objects and words, linked together by intent and desire, and cast that web out into the cosmos to draw your goal to you. Anyone can do spells, and everyone possesses magickal ability. Spellcraft combines the use of imagination, language, and action in a variety of ways, and the way you put it all together will be unique to you.

Spells aren't only about getting what you want, though—they can also be about giving back. You can raise positive energy and send it out into the world, as a way to say "thank you" for all the good things in your own life. You can do spells for other people, too, to aid them in their life journeys. Affirming your blessings and offering assistance to others can help you to draw more blessings to you. You can even do spells to heal the planet, encourage world peace, and other far-reaching objectives.

THE BENEFITS OF SPELLCASTING

Everything in our universe is composed of energy. As you craft and cast spells, you'll come to understand the flow of energy and its presence in and around you. Spellwork teaches you how energy moves, how you can handle it, and how you can direct it into various areas of your life. Once you understand how energy behaves, you can tap into it via different methods—that's what magick is all about.

Spellcraft is a deeply transformative process that touches the magician as well as her environment. Spells and magick are intended to make our lives happier and easier. However, if you think you can use spells to avoid work, forget it—you can't just twitch your nose and make your vacuum cleaner spiff up your home. Spellwork involves effort and dedication, particularly when you first begin, as you acquire new information and explore new techniques. Like everything else, it requires learning the principles and then practicing until you get it right—you must put energy into the equation if you want your outcomes to manifest.

That's not to say spellwork is onerous—anything but! It's a joyful and enlivening experience, one that may actually leave you feeling more vital and content after finishing a spell than you did before you began. Just the act of connecting with parts of yourself to which you ordinarily don't pay much attention can be exhilarating. You discover new strengths and abilities. Plus, knowing that you are linked with the other entities that share your world can give you a sense of belonging to a greater whole, a magickal universe with infinite possibilities.

The Modern Witchcraft Spell Book

Spellwork also helps you gain clarity and purpose. First of all, you must determine a precise goal. Often we think we know what we want, but we rarely take the time to seriously think about how deeply we desire something, and why—or how our lives will change if we get our heart's desire. You have to be completely honest with yourself in order to cast a successful spell, otherwise your hidden agendas may interfere or even materialize. If you do not have a defined goal, you'll end up throwing energy at a vague objective, wasting most of it. If you're confused or ambivalent about your intent, you'll get mixed results. Your spell won't succeed, or will succeed only partially.

By doing spells, you come to know yourself better. You learn to sift through the superficial and get to what really matters—and that benefits every part of your life.

HOW DO SPELLS WORK?

Everything in the world possesses an energy signature of some kind. Organic objects contain more energy than inorganic objects. A piece of wool or silk fabric, for instance, will hold more energy than a piece of polyester. The closer an organic object is to its natural state, the higher its energy. For example, a tree rooted in the wild has more energy than a stack of lumber created from that tree, and a varnished table built from that lumber retains even less of the tree's original energy.

All the energy possessed by these objects reaches out to connect with other energies. A web of energy links the physical and nonphysical worlds. That means you and I and everything else have a connection that enables us to communicate with one another, and, through the power of magick, to work together to consciously create our reality. When we seek to influence a situation by doing spells, we tweak the energy in one location, and that tweak sends ripples all over the web. A common metaphor is that of a spider's web. No matter where a spider sits on her web, when an insect strikes it the tiny shocks travel through all the strands of the web to alert her that she has a visitor for tea. Like the spider's web, strands of energy connect everyone and everything, enabling us to send out our intentions and receive input from our surroundings.

WHAT'S THE DIFFERENCE BETWEEN SPELLCRAFTING AND SPELLCASTING?

Spellcrafting and spellcasting are integrally connected, but they also have certain distinctions. To give a simple explanation, spellcrafting is the practice of fabricating the spell. You think about what you want to accomplish, gather ingredients to include in the spell, write down your objective, figure out the steps you'll take, and so on. Then you put it all together. It's a bit like preparing a recipe—and in fact, culinary recipes can be spells, as you'll learn in Part II of this book.

When you release the energy you've raised during the spellcrafting stage, you "cast" the spell. You send the energy and your intention out into the universe, so that your intention can manifest. Here's another analogy: Crafting the spell is like designing and assembling an automobile, whereas casting the spell is like driving the car. When you cast the spell, you put it to work.

WHERE CAN YOU USE SPELLS?

People use spells in every area of life, for all sorts of reasons. You can use magick spells for just about anything. However, spells for prosperity, love, health, and protection tend to be the most popular. In Part II of this book, you'll find dozens of spells that address these issues, and more.

One reason many of us don't enjoy the riches, well-being, and happiness we could is that we don't feel we deserve them. That lack of self-worth results in lack elsewhere in life. It can also sabotage your magickal workings. Perhaps you've heard of something called the Law of Attraction. This says that you attract what you think about. If you're constantly worrying about how you're going to pay your bills, if you see something you want but say to yourself "I can't afford that," your thoughts are about insufficiency. You think of yourself as being poor. Consequently, you attract poverty and lack. Before you can receive the blessings you desire, you must shift your thinking to prosperity consciousness. You must consider yourself worthy of obtaining your dreams and believe you can attain them.

"If you feel you are poor, you cannot attract prosperity."

ESTHER AND JERRY HICKS, *MONEY, AND THE LAW OF ATTRACTION*

Let's set something straight right now: Spellworking isn't selfish or greedy. When you do a spell to attract money or success or love, you aren't robbing anyone else of those goodies. The universe has plenty for everyone. Fulfilling your basic needs enables you to explore the higher potential of your life—your creativity, your spiritual calling, and so forth. When you no longer have to worry about having food, shelter, and the basic needs in order to survive on planet Earth, you can devote yourself to "loftier" goals that may benefit others as well as you.

As you become more proficient at doing spells, and you begin to see your spells materialize, you'll likely gain more self-confidence. If you're not sure of your abilities yet, it might help to start small. If you can't imagine manifesting $1 million, try a smaller sum, perhaps $100. Don't let yourself get stuck at a level below what's possible, though, because truly anything is within your grasp. The universe can just as easily give you something big as something little—but you have to be open to accepting it.

WHAT'S THE DIFFERENCE BETWEEN A SPELL AND A RITUAL?

Sometimes the words *spell* and *ritual* are used interchangeably, but they are two very different things. Yes, there's some overlap, and that can make things confusing. Think of it this way:

- When you do a spell, you use your mind, emotions, will, and natural powers to bring about an internal or external result.
- When you do a ritual, you perform a series of actions designed for a particular purpose.

In the secular world, we engage in rituals all the time, from dressing for work in the morning to readying ourselves for bed at night. Some secular rituals have traditional aspects, such as donning your favorite sports team's colors at homecoming, painting your face, and packing your cooler with plenty of beer. Spiritual rituals are often performed to honor a higher power or to celebrate your connection with that power, but they may have other purposes as well. A spell can be a part of a ritual, and a lengthy, detailed spell may include ritual actions, as well as interaction with deities.

BASIC STEPS TO SUCCESSFUL SPELLWORK

Although every spell is different, most involve a series of steps, as outlined here, or some version of them. Following these steps not only increases your likelihood of success, it also decreases your chance of mix-ups. An athlete wouldn't run a marathon without stretching first, nor would a surgeon perform a procedure without sterilizing his hands. The same holds true for spellwork. Setting the stage, cleansing your tools, and above all, preparing your mind are important to the success of your spells. Each step of a spell serves a purpose, and they all lead to your desired outcome.

1. Silence all distractions. Turn off the TV, phone, etc. Tell other people who won't be participating in the spell not to bother you—put a Do Not Disturb sign on your door. Put pets in a place where they won't demand your attention or upset your activity. You need to keep your attention focused on your task in order to produce good results. Additionally, when you do a spell, you move from mundane space into magickal space—being jerked back from that magickal place by some outside interference can be jarring, like being shaken out of a peaceful sleep.

2. Establish your intention. Unless you have a clearly defined reason for doing a spell, don't bother. It's simply a waste of time and energy, and your efforts may go awry. Write down your intention—this helps clarify your objective and starts the process of moving it out of your mind, into physical form. If you'll be working with other people, discuss your intention together beforehand so everyone understands what you're doing and why. It's essential that you're all in agreement and that you all focus on the same intention; otherwise, you might get mixed results.

The Modern Witchcraft Spell Book

3. Compose your spell. Think about your desired outcome and what energies you wish to harness in order to help you achieve this outcome. Write down what you'll do in your spell and the steps with which you'll proceed. If you plan to use an affirmation or incantation, make sure you either memorize it or write it down. (You'll learn more about this in Chapter 5.) If you'll be working with other people, go over the steps and details beforehand, so everyone is in accord and feels comfortable with his or her role.

4. Collect all the ingredients necessary for your spell. Cleanse each item, either by washing it with mild soap and water or by "smudging" it in the smoke of burning sage or incense. Bring all the objects you'll use into the space where you'll perform your spell. Ritual tools should have been consecrated beforehand (you'll learn more about these tools in Chapter 6). If you'll work with other spellcasters, decide whose tools will be used in the spell and who will wield them.

5. Establish your spellworking space. First, cleanse the area where you'll perform your spell. You can do this by smudging it with smoke from burning sage or incense or by sweeping it with a broom or both. Sometimes imagining the area filled with pure white light may be enough. Invite everyone who will participate to enter the space, and then cast a circle around it. (We'll discuss this in depth in Chapter 3.) A magick circle provides an energetic barrier that keeps unwanted energies out and holds desired energies in.

6. Shift your consciousness. Light a candle or incense, meditate, or do whatever helps you shift your thinking from mundane to magickal. From this point on, try not to let any ordinary thoughts intrude into your elevated mental state. If you're working with other people, don't talk unless you're chanting an affirmation or performing another verbal part of your spell.

7. Raise energy. Some people do this by chanting, humming, drumming, breathing deeply, or dancing—do what feels right to you. Envision yourself drawing energy up from the earth and into your body; also draw energy from the heavens down into your body, and let them blend within you. You'll sense your awareness change—you might feel more energized, calm, aware, centered, sensitive, tingly, or something else. If you're working with other people, allow your individual

energies to merge for the term of the spell. (We'll discuss this more in later chapters.)

8. If you choose, invite other entities to participate in your spell. Angelic presences, spirit guides and guardians, totem animals, ancestors, elementals, and other nonphysical beings can provide protection and assistance during spellwork. (We'll talk more about working with spirit beings in Chapter 7.)

9. Perform your spell, according to the plan you designed earlier.

10. After completing your spell, release the entities who've assisted you (if any) and thank them.

11. Open the circle. (You'll learn how in Chapter 3.) Send the energy you've raised during your spellwork toward your goal, and trust that it will materialize at the proper time, in the proper way.

12. Dismantle your magickal space. Extinguish the candles, collect your tools and any other items you brought into the circle, etc. Store your tools in a safe place until you choose to work with them again.

13. The final step is manifestation—this is when you achieve your goal.

In your book of shadows (your personal journal of spells), write down what you did and what ingredients/tools you used when you performed the spell, as well as what you felt, sensed, thought, witnessed, and so on. If you're working with other spellcasters, you may wish to discuss what transpired, how you felt about the spell and its enactment, and what (if anything) you might do differently in the future.

The Modern Witchcraft Spell Book

Chapter 2

TAPPING MAGICKAL POWER

What does it mean to practice magick? When we speak of magick, we mean the transformation that occurs when a witch, wizard, shaman, or other magick worker uses his or her power to shape energy, in order to accomplish an objective in the physical or nonphysical world (or both). When a witch does a magick spell, she doesn't send sparks flying from her fingertips, nor does she levitate objects and hurl them through space—that's pure Hollywood. Instead, she attunes her own innate abilities with the forces of nature to elicit a series of controlled coincidences that will achieve her desired result. She moves, bends, or otherwise alters the flow of energy in the universe to bring about a condition that will benefit her or someone else.

Each person who decides to take up the practice of magick has reasons for doing so. Before you begin performing spells, spend some time thinking about why spellcasting is important to you and what you hope to achieve by engaging in this practice. Write your thoughts in your book of shadows—putting something in writing helps you to clarify your thoughts. Begin to define what you believe. Do you seek out magick as a way to escape from the mundane aspects of life? Are you mainly concerned about making changes in your personal life (love, career, money)? Or do you want to deepen your spiritual connection to the universe? Do you intend to obtain practical results or to enhance your intuition? Most likely, your goals will include a combination of all these things, and maybe more.

The Law of Three

Ethical spellworkers abide by what's known as the "law of three." This means that whatever intention and energy someone sends out returns, like a boomerang, to the sender threefold. This is a strong deterrent against mischief, manipulation, or other deceptive practices.

CONSCIOUSLY CREATING CHANGE

It's been said that the only constant is change. We observe change all around us, all the time. The rising sun changes night to day; the setting sun changes day to night. Wind changes the face of the mountain. Rain changes the depth of the river, which wears away the rocks to carve the valley. Fire changes substance to ash. Planet Earth is constantly shifting, spinning, revolving, and renewing itself.

The purpose of doing magick is to create change intentionally. When you cast a spell, you bring about a change in some facet of your life and the world around you. When you cast a circle (as you'll learn to do in Chapter 3), you change a room or a grove of trees into a sacred temple. When you build an altar, you change a table or other surface into the stage upon which you interact with other forces and entities. When you consecrate a magick tool, you change an ordinary stick or wineglass into an instrument of Divine Will.

You possess the power to change just about anything in your life. As quantum physics has demonstrated, when you focus your attention on something, your energy influences the behavior of the molecules that you are watching (even though you can't actually see them). Focusing on something causes molecules to collect in the area where you direct your attention. What this means is, you quite literally change whatever you observe. That's magick! The goal—and the challenge—is to use magick with conscious awareness and intent. Spells are one way to do this.

WHERE DOES MAGICKAL POWER ORIGINATE?

We live in a magickal universe. Everything you see—and don't see—is imbued with magickal potential. We've been taught to believe that the things around us are material, tangible, and immutable substances, but none of that is true. A tree, a rock, the chair you're sitting on are all composed of energy. As I've said before, our world is surrounded by an energetic matrix that connects everything to everything else. This matrix, or cosmic web, not only envelops earth, it permeates all things that exist here, and it extends throughout the solar system and beyond. The web pulses with subtle vibrations, which witches and other sensitive individuals can feel. Regardless of whether you are consciously aware of these vibrations, you are affected by them—and your own energetic vibrations continually affect the matrix.

Let's talk some more about the Law of Attraction, because it's a fundamental part of magickal practice and spellwork. According to Esther and Jerry Hicks, whose bestselling books have done a great deal to popularize this ancient concept, "Each and every component that makes up your life experience is drawn to you by the powerful Law of Attraction's response to the thoughts you think and the story you tell about your life." This means that your ideas contain magnetic power, and that you're already bringing to yourself the outcomes you'll experience—even if you don't realize it.

What you get is what you see. The ideas and beliefs you hold in your mind are the source of what happens to you. They are the seeds from which your reality grows. Your thoughts, words, and deeds are at the root of your health, wealth, and happiness—or your illness, poverty, and misery. That's not meant to cast blame but to help you understand the amazing power you have at your fingertips.

In magickal work, learning to harness and direct your thoughts is essential to creating successful outcomes. Look around at your life circumstances. If you don't like something, know that you possess the power to change it, by first changing your thoughts.

Energy Signatures

Everything in the world emits energy of some kind, and everything has a unique energy "signature." Sometimes a signature is described as corresponding to a particular level of vibration. Higher vibrational levels usually are considered more spiritual and closer to the deities; lower vibrations indicate something more material.

YOUR PERSONAL ENERGY CENTERS

Just as your physical body has internal organs that enable it to perform various tasks necessary for survival, you also have nonphysical "organs" or energy centers that play an important part in your well-being. Asian health and healing practices, such as acupuncture, ayurvedic medicine, Reiki, and yoga, deal with the movement of energy through your body—especially as it relates to these dynamic energy centers known as the "chakras." The word *chakra* means "wheel" because to sensitive people who can perceive them these orb-like energy centers resemble spinning wheels or spirals. However, most individuals can't perceive them, nor can they be quantified using conventional medicine's tools.

Although many chakras exist throughout the body, we're primarily concerned with seven major chakras that roughly align vertically from the base of your spine to the top of your head. Each serves a particular function as a locus of energy that nourishes your body, mind, and spirit. When your chakras are in balance, your intuitive and psychic abilities are at their strongest, and you can draw upon their energy to work magick effectively. You'll find a number of spells in Part II of this book that involve working with the energy of the chakras.

Kundalini: The Mystical Serpent

According to mystical Eastern wisdom, the divine essence of all the chakras is *kundalini*. Kundalini is depicted as a serpent coiled around herself three and a half times. The serpent sleeps at the base of the spine and awakens (through yoga, breath work, or other practices) with a rattle or a hiss. She slowly uncoils herself and begins her ascent, traveling up through each chakra center, opening and activating it as she goes. Each major chakra is associated with a color and a significant symbol (which are all variations on the lotus flower). Use these symbols as guides to understanding and integrating these vital energies, so that you may experience the benefits. You'll find lots of pictures of the chakras online and in books, to help you connect with them further.

The Root Chakra

The root chakra is located at the base of the spine and is linked with the color red. This energy center deals with all issues pertaining to survival—it is your connection to the earth. Many fight-or-flight responses and animal instincts are stored here. The root chakra is also concerned with security, your sense of self, and your confidence. When you activate the root chakra you embrace your primal nature, as an integrated and necessary part of your higher self.

This chakra also affects your interactions with the material world. If your root chakra is balanced, you are likely to feel secure with your place in the world and your ability to cope with any hardships that may come your way. Blockages in the root chakra, however, may lead to feelings of inadequacy, insecurity, and a lack of self-confidence, which can interfere with everything you embark on, including spellwork. You can strengthen your root chakra by meditating and envisioning a glowing red ball of energy at the base of your spine, continually growing brighter and stronger.

The Sacral Chakra

Located just below the navel, the sacral chakra is associated with sex, desire, pleasure, and fulfillment. Its color is orange. Your carnal instincts reside here, in this realm of procreation and sensuality. When you open and balance your sacral chakra, you accept yourself as a sexual being who seeks pleasure. Obviously, this chakra affects spells you do for love. In addition to its correlation with sexuality, the sacral chakra impacts other kinds of desire as well. Your passionate hopes, dreams, and aspirations dwell here, too.

If your sacral chakra is balanced, you are likely to feel comfortable with your sexuality. You may also be adept at understanding and expressing your own needs on many levels, and you can find ways to make sure your needs are met. A deficiency or blockage in the sacral chakra may lead to excessive inhibition, as well as feelings of discomfort regarding sexuality and perhaps pleasure in general. Consequently, you might limit your ability as a creative being and as a spellworker, for doing magick spells is a creative endeavor. When your sacral chakra is balanced, you easily connect with your own needs and desires and your ability to attract what you seek. Visualize a spinning vortex of bright orange light just below your navel to activate your sacral chakra.

The Solar Plexus Chakra

The solar plexus chakra, located about halfway between your navel and your heart, is the center of your personal power. Its color is yellow. Its energy enables you to actualize your personal gifts and talents. Your willpower resides here, and when this chakra is functioning optimally, you take charge of your life and exercise your power—in the mundane world as well as the magickal one. When you open your solar plexus chakra, you take responsibility for your choices and feel confident acting upon them.

If your solar plexus chakra is balanced, you feel comfortable expressing your unique abilities. You use this chakra's energy to produce positive results for yourself and others, without fear or reluctance. In spellwork, your personal talents come to fruition, bringing you a greater sense of self-worth and helping you attain your goals. To strengthen this chakra, envision a brilliant yellow light, like sunshine, glowing there and radiating out into the world.

The Heart Chakra

The heart chakra, as its name implies, is located in the middle of the chest near your heart. Its color is green. This chakra deals with issues that pertain to the emotions, especially your ability to love and be loved, and obviously it plays an important role in love spells. It serves as the link between your physical body and your spiritual identity. The heart chakra is involved not only with romantic love but also love of self and love of community: family, friends, and humanity in general. It also connects you to nature and the spirits with whom you interact, whether or not you are aware of them.

When your heart chakra is open and balanced, you experience love without walls and can accept your own vulnerability without fear. Blockages in the heart chakra can lead to feelings of unworthiness, mistrust, and loneliness. People who have had their hearts broken often distance themselves from the heart chakra, saying things such as "I will never allow anyone to get that close to me again" or "No one will ever get the chance to hurt me like that again." To open this chakra, meditate and imagine spiraling green light all around your heart, sending forth love and receiving love as well.

The Throat Chakra

At the base of your throat, near the hollow where your collarbones meet, you'll find the throat chakra. Its color is light blue. All matters of communication relate to this energy center, as well as how you interact with other beings in the world around you and in the higher planes of consciousness. The manner by which you express your thoughts and speak your own truth is also affected by the throat chakra. Because many spells involve affirmations, incantations, or other verbalizations, this chakra affects the success of your spells.

If your throat chakra is blocked or imbalanced, you may take a dogmatic approach to discussing ideas or beliefs. Perhaps you talk excessively without listening or get caught up in arguing. Or you might be afraid to speak about your ideas or to share your talents with others for fear of criticism. To balance this chakra, imagine a beautiful, light-blue glow swirling at the base of your throat.

The Third Eye Chakra

The third eye or "ajna" chakra is located at your forehead where your eyebrows come together at the top of your nose. Its color is indigo. This is the site of psychic awareness, where matters pertaining to your intuition or "sixth sense" reside. It allows you to experience your spiritual nature through clairvoyance (seeing the unseen), memories of past lives, empathy (feeling what others feel), telepathy (accessing the thoughts of another), and astral travel (entering into nonphysical realms where the physical body cannot go).

When your third eye chakra is open and balanced, you experience your connection with other realms and may find you can communicate easily (intuitively) with beings who reside there. In magickal work, you can receive spiritual guidance and wisdom from higher sources—you may even be able to divine the future. A blockage or imbalance in this chakra may lead you to reject your own psychic gifts out of fear or skepticism. To activate your ajna chakra, picture the indigo light of the sky at night emanating from your third eye.

The Crown Chakra

Located at or just above the top of your head, this chakra is associated with the color purple, though some people see it as white. All spiritual matters pertaining to your soul's existence dwell here. The crown chakra serves as a portal through which you receive spiritual guidance and wisdom. A balanced crown chakra allows you to communicate with god/desses and divine beings on other levels of existence and to receive aid from them in magickal work.

When you activate and balance your crown chakra, your ego falls away; you live in a state of acceptance and assimilation with the Divine, a place beyond desire. You experience a sense of oneness with all beings. Because you know your spirit is indestructible, you fear nothing, not even physical death. An imbalance in the crown chakra can cause you to feel lost, alone, cut off from your Source and the higher forces that exist around you. Or you might suffer from delusions of grandeur. To bring this chakra into balance, visualize a brilliant, regal purple light emanating from the top of your head, flowing over you and through you, connecting you to All That Is.

CREATIVE VISUALIZATION

In the late 1970s, author Shakti Gawain brought the concept of creative visualization into widespread public awareness. But witches and other magickal practitioners had long known that visualization fuels magick and precedes manifestation. When you're doing a spell, a picture truly is worth a thousand words.

Creative visualization involves forming a mental picture of the result you intend to manifest. Don't think about the problem or condition you wish to change—instead, focus on the end result you seek. For instance, if your goal is to heal a broken leg, don't think about the injury; instead, envision the leg strong and healthy.

Images possess more power than words. Advertisers know this very well—just watch a commercial for some sort of drug, in which the pictures show happy, healthy people while the voice-over describes all the drug's unpleasant side effects. The viewer's mind reacts to the pictures rather than the words. Because images have such a strong impact, witches incorporate lots of visual and sensory components into magick spells, as well as words.

Imagination is at the heart of a spell. If you can't conceive of a situation or state of being, you won't be able to attain it. When you imagine the possibilities of what you may be able to create, you plant the first seeds. Remember how, as a child, you had fun letting your imagination run free? It's time to do that again. Give yourself permission to dream big. Enrich your mental images with lots of color and action—clear, vivid images generate faster and more satisfactory results than bland ones.

Try this exercise with a friend to explore your ability to form mental images:

1. Silence all distractions (phone, TV, etc.).
2. Sit in a comfortable place and close your eyes.
3. Ask your friend to say aloud a series of words, one by one, such as "apple," "horse," "campfire," "sailboat," or "ski chalet."
4. Notice the pictures that pop into your mind. Do you see a shiny red apple? A sleek, chestnut-colored horse with white stockings? A blazing fire shooting sparks into the night sky?

5. Choose one of those images, and let it spin out into something more. Do you envision a racehorse galloping toward the finish line? Girl Scouts seated around a campfire roasting marshmallows?
6. Now switch places, so your friend can exercise his imagination while you give him verbal "cues."
7. Record your images and impressions in your book of shadows.

Creative visualization will improve your psychic abilities as well. Once you learn to clear your psyche of all that useless clutter and chatter that take up space in your mind, you'll find your innate creativity can express itself. Furthermore, you can begin to form mental images that are in line with your purposes and that will attract the outcomes you desire.

What Is a Book of Shadows?

A book of shadows is a witch's personal journal of his or her magickal experiences. Here you keep track of your spells, rituals, and other things related to your development as a magician. It's like a cook's collection of recipes. Often you'll hear the words *grimoire* and *book of shadows* used interchangeably, although some differences existed in earlier times. Grimoires served as guidebooks that described spells and rituals. A book of shadows might also include its author's musings or insights related to a spell, as well as her dreams, feelings, and other asides.

LEARNING TO SENSE ENERGY

Magick spells draw upon the energies within you and around you. If you're going to become a successful spellworker, you'll benefit from learning to tap into the vast storehouse of energy that's available to you. Although energy currents flow in and around us all the time, invisibly wafting through our environment, most people don't pay attention to them. However, you can develop an awareness of them, and doing so will enhance your spellwork. Try these exercises to hone your ability to sense energy:

- Enter a building you've never been in before. Notice your reactions. Do you feel comfortable, welcomed, at ease? Or do you experience apprehension or hesitation? Do you want to continue further into the building, or withdraw? (This relates to an ancient Chinese magickal system known as *feng shui.*)
- Go to several different places, perhaps high on a hilltop and then near a body of water and finally deep in the woods. Spend some time sensing the "vibes" there. How do you feel in these different spots? Consider not just the obvious things, such as wind or sun or dampness, but also your personal reactions. Do you feel more enlivened in one place or another? Do you feel calm or agitated in a particular spot? Even if your impressions seem weird, don't discount them.
- Now go to several different places in a town or city. What do you experience there? How do you react to the faster pace? Does the energy seem more chaotic than it did in the natural places you visited? Do you find the energy invigorating or stressful? Exciting or draining?
- Go outside at night and look up at the sky. What do you see and sense? Many people are afraid of the dark—are you? And if so, why? In the world of magick, nighttime relates to mystery, the subconscious, and the realm beyond our everyday activities. In some magickal traditions, nighttime is the Goddess's time, when the feminine force is most active. Pay attention to your own experiences and remember to note them in your book of shadows.
- Go outside at dawn and again at dusk. These interim times, between day and night, are known as liminal zones. All around you, things are changing. Because change is essential to spellwork, you can align yourself with these transitions to perform powerful magick. Pay attention to the energetic shifts you sense as day and night switch places.

In Chapter 8, we'll look more closely at the energies inherent in the moon's phases, the earth's cycle around the sun, and other passages that can enhance or hamper your spellwork. You'll also learn how to time your spells to take advantage of the powers of nature and the cosmos that are available to you at various times throughout the year.

Chapter 3

A PLACE FOR SPELLWORKING

We've all had the experience of entering a place of reverence and sanctuary, whether it's a church or temple, a meditation room at a yoga center, or a grove of trees in a peaceful, natural setting. As soon as you step inside this special space, you sense a shift in the energy. You may feel serene, safe, suddenly removed from the busyness outside, or at one with something larger than yourself.

When you do spells or rituals, you want to go to a spot where you feel this sort of heightened awareness, connection, and peace. You need to leave the mundane world behind temporarily and slip into the world of magick. Creating sacred space is just as important as preparing yourself for spellwork. Maybe you're fortunate enough to have a place to call your sanctuary—a room in your home or a lovely, private spot in your yard. However, any place where you practice magick is your temple, and any place you treat with reverence is sacred space.

Your personal temple needn't be elaborate or large, like the ancient and awe-inspiring religious structures in India that occupy many acres. You can create a special area for magickal and spiritual practice in a corner of a room, on your back porch, or on the roof of your apartment building. In fact, if you live with people who might not understand or accept your beliefs, you may decide it's best to use a low-key, unobtrusive place to do your magickal work. You can place a vase of flowers, a candle, a colorful scarf, and a pretty stone on a shelf or dresser to designate your special place—you know the significance behind these everyday items, but no one else will.

BETWEEN THE WORLDS

When you prepare yourself to cast a spell or enact a ritual, you suspend your everyday concept of reality for a period of time. You expand your perception of the universe and your place in it, and get in touch with energies beyond your own. By entering the space and time "between the worlds," as it's often called, you can connect with the spirits who reside there. You acknowledge their presence by inviting them into your sacred space (we'll talk about this more in Chapter 7). You agree to accept physical manifestations of their divine presence. And you agree to suspend your sense of disbelief, in order to accept that magick and psychic experiences are indeed possible and even desirable.

At first, this may be difficult, as the rational mind often requires some type of tangible "proof" that a spiritual experience has occurred. This is where trust in yourself and the entities you work with comes in. Often your interactions will be subtle, but you'll learn in time to recognize gentle signs. You probably won't hear a clap of thunder to assure you that the goddesses and gods have acknowledged your work. Then again, you just might.

The Distinction Between Sacred Space and a Magick Circle

What makes sacred space different from a magick circle? A circle is a consciously constructed space that partially overlaps both our material world and the divine world. The resulting area is said to be "between the worlds," not wholly in one or the other. Sacred space is a place of peace and calm, but it is not necessarily between the worlds. Sacred space goes into the circle, or it can simply exist on its own.

CREATING SACRED SPACE

The purpose of defining and consecrating a sacred space is to give yourself a dedicated realm in which to perform magick and ritual, where you can move beyond your ordinary world when you so choose. You are, in essence, raising a temple (though not necessarily a brick-and-mortar one) for meditation, worship, divination, spellcasting, or any other aspect of magickal practice you wish to do here. You can create a more or less permanent sacred space or a temporary one, depending on your intentions and circumstances.

Cleansing Your Sacred Space

Once you've determined the location of your sacred space, take a broom and sweep the area thoroughly to clear away dust, dirt, and clutter. This is what witches really use brooms for, not to fly through the sky. After you finish physically sweeping the area, focus on cleansing the psychic space. In this way, you remove unwanted energies or influences, any "bad vibes" that might linger there.

Begin in the east and work your way counterclockwise around the room, in a circular fashion. Sweep the air, from the floor up to as high as you can comfortably reach. When you have gone around your area three times, lay the broom on the floor inside the circle and visualize all the negative energy breaking up and dissolving.

Some spellworkers also like to "smudge" the area with the smoke from burning sage. Light a sage wand/bundle (available at New Age shops and online) or a stick of sage incense. Walk in a circle, starting in the east, letting the smoke waft through the area. Now stand in the center of your space and feel the fresh, light, clean energy around you.

Dedicating Your Sacred Space

The next step is to dedicate your sacred space. You can begin by anointing the room or outdoor area you've chosen with frankincense essential oil (or another oil you prefer). Just put a little dab in each corner, starting in the east and moving clockwise around the space, creating a cross within a circle. This symbol represents the balance of female and male energies, the circle of creation, the four directions, and the four elements (about which we'll talk more later).

You may also opt to place a stone or crystal that has meaning for you at each of the four compass directions. If your sacred space is outdoors, you can bury the stones in the ground. Or you might like to design symbols that signify peace, holiness, protection, power, etc. and position them in your space. Some people display images of beloved deities in their sacred spaces. If you wish, you can create an elaborate ritual for dedicating your space—it is up to you.

Protecting Your Sacred Space

After you've finished setting up your sacred space, you'll want to protect it from intrusive energies. If you've designated your home or another building as sacred space, consider the following:

- Empower a mirror to deflect negative energy and hang it on your front door, facing outward (this is also a popular feng shui "cure"). Any disruptive energy that comes toward you will bounce back, away from your space.
- Bury protective stones such as onyx, hematite, or peridot under your doorstep, porch, or steps. (You can obtain these stones at your local New Age store.)
- Put a bunch of fresh basil in a pot with two quarts of water and simmer for ten minutes. Then strain out the basil (save it for other spells) and wash your doorstep with the basil-infused water.

- Hang a protective symbol on your door or near the entrance of your home: a pentagram, a Pennsylvania Dutch hex sign, or another image you associate with protection.
- Using saltwater, draw pentagrams or other protection symbols on the doors and windows of your home.
- Hang braids or wreaths of garlic, onions, and/or hot peppers in your home (don't eat them).
- Set a clove of garlic on each of your windowsills to absorb any negative energy before it can enter your home. Toss the old cloves and replace them with fresh ones on each new moon.
- Hang an iron horseshoe above your front door, with the open end turned up.

If you can't or choose not to consider your entire home (or another building) as sacred space, you can adapt the previous list according to your area. For example, if you have designated a portion of a room:

- Place a stone associated with protection there.
- Lay dried basil leaves in your sacred space.
- Position or draw a pentagram or other protective symbol there.
- Sprinkle some sea salt or spritz saltwater in the area.
- Set a clove of garlic in your space.

As you go about any daily routines that take place in your sacred space—especially if you've dedicated your entire home—be mindful of the energies around you. To attract positive energy, dust, mop, wash, and wipe countertops using a clockwise motion. To dispel unwanted energies, use a counterclockwise motion.

SETTING UP YOUR ALTAR

In my previous book *The Modern Guide to Witchcraft* I discussed in depth the process of setting up an altar. Here I'll offer a condensed version. Your altar is your basic "workbench" where you will do magick—just as a carpenter cuts, sands, glues, and nails at his workbench. It provides a focal point when you're casting spells, performing rites and rituals, meditating, communing with deities, or conducting any other magickal practices you may wish to engage in, either alone or with other people. You can set up a permanent altar or a temporary one within your sacred space, depending on your circumstances and preferences.

What Constitutes an Altar?

You can fashion an altar from just about anything—your intention is what's important and your understanding that the altar you've established is sacred. Perhaps you'd like to designate a handsome piece of furniture as your altar. Or, you can simply lay a pretty piece of cloth on a shelf, TV table, or cardboard box. If you choose to work outside, you could dedicate a large stone or a tree stump as your altar. If you decide to erect a temporary altar for spellworking, dismantle it when you're finished doing your spell.

Many people display their magick tools on their altars and store them there when not in use. Whether you opt to leave your tools in place more or less permanently or can only do this temporarily, display items that represent all four elements, for balance: earth, air, fire, and water. This could mean placing your pentagram, athame (ritual dagger), wand, and chalice on your altar. (We'll talk more about these tools in Chapter 6.) Or you could set a crystal there to signify earth, incense for air, a candle for fire, and a small bowl or vase of water for water. You can position anything on your altar that holds sacred or positive meaning for you: gemstones, statues of deities, images of totem animals, fresh flowers, etc., as well as the objects that you'll use in your spellwork. The most important thing is that you feel a sense of peace, joy, safety, and personal power when you do spells in your sacred space. Your altar serves as an anchor and a center of focus within that space.

Seasonal Altars

You may enjoy decorating your altar to celebrate the changing seasons or to mark special holidays, such as the eight sabbats (discussed in Chapter 8). Doing this will help you to attune yourself to the energies of the time and keep your altar looking fresh.

Positioning Your Altar

There's no right or wrong place within your sacred space to position your altar. Often the location of your altar depends on how much room you have, who will perform spells and rituals there (just you or other people as well), and what type of magick you'll do. Some people like to put the altar in the center of the space, which is convenient if a number of spellcasters will be doing magick together. Others prefer to set the altar in the north or the east. You can move your altar to different spots at different times of the year, or according to the moon's changing phases. Depending on your space, you may decide to erect more than one altar, perhaps a main one and smaller ones at each of the four directions. It's really up to you.

Directional Altars

If you opt to set up an altar at each of the four compass directions or "quarters," consider decorating each one to correspond to the nature of that direction. Witches associate the color yellow with the east, red with the south, blue with the west, and green with the north. You could put candles, flowers, fabric, gemstones, or other objects of the appropriate colors on your altars to signify their energies and enhance your awareness of your place within the whole.

Remember to cleanse everything before you bring it into your sacred space and place it on your altar(s). You can do this by washing items with mild soap and water, smudging them with the smoke of burning sage or incense, gently rubbing them with a piece of citrine (yellow quartz), or envisioning them surrounded and suffused with pure white light.

CASTING A CIRCLE

Nearly every book you read about magick and spellwork will discuss the importance of circle casting and offer suggestions for how to do it. Circles embody a wealth of symbolism, including wholeness, unity, completion, protection, eternity, and power. Some people say a circle protects those within it from evil forces, and although that may be true, it's not the main reason for casting a circle. Many traditions recommend doing magick within a psychic circle, for various reasons:

- A circle erects an energetic fence around the place where you do your magickal workings. This fence keeps unwanted energies out of your sacred space, so they can't disrupt or interfere with what you're doing.
- A circle contains the positive energy you raise during your spell or ritual. It holds and intensifies your power and intent until you're ready to release them into the larger world.
- If you are working with other people, a circle unites and enhances your energies, so that the group's power becomes greater than that of each individual within it.
- A circle brings you into closer contact with the sacred, moving you out of the mundane world temporarily and into the realm of magick and mystery. You realize that your actions are separated from your everyday existence and that increases the intensity of your focus. During the time you abide within the circle, you occupy a holy zone, nearer to the gods, goddesses, and spirits who can aid, guide, and protect you while you perform your spellwork.

As I've said before, casting a circle begins as an act of faith, to an extent—you *believe* the circle is there. Over time, or perhaps even on your very first attempt, you'll sense that the energy within the circle is very different from the energy outside it.

Preparing to Cast a Circle

Before you begin the physical part of casting a circle, it's important to ready the space where you'll erect your magick circle. This means cleansing it physically and psychically, just as you would any sacred space. Clear out anything that doesn't play a part in the spell or ritual you'll enact here. Sweep away old energies with a broom, as discussed earlier. Smudge the area with burning sage or incense.

Remove any distractions. Turn off all electronics: TV, phone, etc. Make sure people who won't be involved in your spell or ritual know not to disturb you. Put pets in a safe place where they won't interrupt. Cleanse all tools, spell ingredients, and other items that you'll use in your magick. Bring them into the area where you'll be working.

Ready yourself and all other participants. Go to the bathroom and tend to any personal needs, so you won't have to interrupt the spell/ritual once you get started. You may want to spend some time meditating or chanting to calm your mind and shift your focus. Smudge yourself and everyone else, to remove unwanted energies before entering the sacred space. You may wish to anoint participants with "holy" water, essential oils, or another substance that serves both to purify and to unite everyone involved.

Circle Casting 101

The ritual of casting a circle can be as simple or as complex as you want (or need) it to be. Some magick groups engage in elaborate and intricate ceremonies that contain many precise steps and ingredients. But you can also cast a perfectly effective circle by simply envisioning the area surrounded by a wall of pure white light. For many years, I worked within a large stone labyrinth that I'd built in the woods behind my house; it served as both my sacred space and a permanent magick circle. The directions offered here are suggestions only—feel free to design your own method according to your own preferences.

1. Gather all participants into the area where you'll be working, so that once you've cast the circle everyone will be inside it. After you've entered this sacred space, do not talk unless what you say is part of the ritual or spell.
2. Walk around the perimeter (often three times) of your intended workspace, beginning in the east and moving clockwise until you've made a complete circle and come back to your starting point. If you wish, draw the circle using a ceremonial sword, wand, or athame. Delineate the outer edge of the circle by holding the wand or blade parallel to the ground and pointing it outward. This physical act defines the circle in your mind.
3. To expand the circle so that it exists both in the physical realm and in the spiritual one, visualize energy being channeled into the space defined by the circle. Then expand it further, so that you envision a sphere of energy that encompasses you above, below, and around. With your imagination, you draw up energy from the earth and draw

down energy from the sky, blending them so that the combination fills the space.

4. If you choose to invite any spirits, guides, deities, ancestors, etc. to join in your spell/ritual, now is the time to call upon them. We'll address this practice in Chapter 7.

Once the circle is cast, no one should leave or enter it. If it becomes absolutely necessary to admit or dismiss someone, use your athame (or your hand) to "cut" an opening in the circle in the shape of a door, so that the person can enter or depart. Seal the opening afterward.

Opening the Circle

After you've finished your ritual or spellwork, you must open the circle so that the energy you've raised within it can flow out and materialize in the greater world. Basically, you'll reverse the steps you took to cast the circle.

1. If you've called upon any god/desses, angels, spirits, totems, or other nonphysical entities, thank them for their assistance and release them (we'll talk more about this in Chapter 7).

2. If you used a ritual athame, wand, or sword to draw the circle, take it up again and hold it with the point facing out, as you did to cast the circle. Retrace the path you used to create the circle, only in reverse— walk counterclockwise (three times if that's what you did to cast the circle) until you've removed all the psychic energy with which you built the circle.

3. Envision the magickal energy you raised during your spell/ritual flowing out into the universe, where it will manifest in accordance with your intentions. Sense that all is as it should be and trust that your objectives will come about in harmony with your will and that of Divine Will.

4. Extinguish candles and/or other flames. Gather up your tools (unless you prefer to leave them in your sacred space) and anything else you brought into the sacred space for the purposes of this spell/ritual. All participants can now leave the circle and return to their ordinary world.

In a nutshell, that's it. You can adapt this very basic pattern to make it more personal, embellish it to give it more drama, or interpret it as your own beliefs dictate. In later chapters, we'll talk more about other possibilities you may want to consider including. I also encourage you to read other books and to use your creativity to devise ways to enrich your circle casting to make it more meaningful for you. There are probably as many options as there are magickal workers—you're limited only by your imagination.

Chapter 4

NATURE'S MAGICK

Today, few people use eye of newt and toe of frog in spells. They're more likely to choose everyday ingredients they can find in any supermarket or New Age store—or better yet, in the natural environment. Using objects from nature is a wonderful way to enhance your connection with Mother Earth and to increase the power of your spells by adding the energies of plants, stones, etc. Since ancient times, witches, shamans, sorcerers, and other magick workers have looked to nature for spell materials. They used herbs and flowers to make healing potions, salves, poultices, and tonics. Gemstones and crystals provided protection, augmented personal powers, and attracted blessings. The natural world still provides a cornucopia of plants, minerals, and other treasures that you can use in your own magickal workings.

Many of the spells in Part II of this book include botanicals and/or gemstones. At the beginning of most chapters, you'll find lists that recommend the best plants, herbs, essential oils, and stones to use for specific types of spells.

SYMPATHETIC MAGICK

The basic philosophy of sympathetic magick is quite simple: like attracts like. This means that in spellwork, an item can serve as a representative or stand-in for another item that's similar to it in some way. It also means that the similarities are not coincidental and that they signify a connection—physical, spiritual, energetic, or otherwise—between the two items. Ginseng root, for example, resembles the human body, a similarity that some healers believe contributes to ginseng's medicinal properties. When you do spells, you can use associations between objects in order to make your spells more effective. In some instances, you may be aware of these connections; in other cases, the understanding happens at a subconscious level.

Because similarities exist between items, you can often substitute one ingredient for another in a spell. For example, a sunflower represents the energy of the sun, so if you're doing a spell that calls for solar power you can use sunflower seeds or petals to represent that power. If you're doing a love spell, you could use a pink rose or a piece of rose quartz—both resonate with the vibration of love. The energy of the flower is quicker, the stone's more enduring; however, either can play a role in a love spell.

Symbolism Exercise

Take a moment to consider how you form associations. Because your mind is the most important factor in magick, the mental images you hold are tremendously important when you perform spells. What do the words in the following list signify for you? What ideas and connections do they conjure up in your mind?

- Rose
- Snake
- Diamond
- Silk
- Horse
- Cactus
- Waterfall

- Apple
- Box
- Arrow

Most likely, your mind instantly produced a picture of the object. Beyond that, though, your imagination probably spun off in other directions and started making associations. For example, the word *diamond* may have triggered images of marriage or wealth. The word *horse* may have brought to mind thoughts of freedom, power, grace, speed, or beauty. Because your subconscious just naturally forms associations of this kind, you can make it work for you in spellcasting by choosing objects that symbolize your intentions.

Throughout this book, you'll see many examples of sympathetic magick at work. Some of the spells in Part II recommend choosing objects that hold significance for you or relate to your goals, and incorporating them into your spell. As you grow in knowledge and experience as a spellworker, you'll just naturally start making connections of this type.

Color Connections

Colors surround and influence us in countless ways, whether or not we realize it. That's why colors play such an important role in spellwork. Green is often used for money spells in the United States, because U.S. paper money is green on one side. In nature, green also makes us think of new growth and healthy plants. These are powerful associations. Yellow reminds us of sunshine, warmth, and happiness, so magick workers use this color for spells to attract good luck and joy. We associate the color red with passion; hence, love spells often include red flowers and red gemstones. In sympathetic magick, what "seems like" often "is." The underlying message is to trust your instincts—if something intuitively seems right to you, go with it.

MAGICKAL BOTANICALS

Many plants possess medicinal and healing properties, but for our purposes, we'll focus here on the metaphysical attributes of herbs and flowers. The category "botanicals" includes flowers, herbs, trees, shrubs, fruits and vegetables, and all sorts of other plants. In spellcraft, each has its purpose and value. In fact, plants are probably the most frequently used ingredients in spells of all kinds.

Choosing and Preparing Botanicals

Five thousand years ago, the Chinese emperor Shen Nung compiled the earliest known herbal reference book. Although the original text no longer exists, many later herbals evolved from this compilation. Some 2,000 years before the birth of Christ, the Egyptians and Sumerians kept records regarding the properties and applications of plants. The Egyptians used herbs extensively for cosmetic, medicinal, and embalming purposes.

As the Mediterranean trade routes grew and flourished, the use of herbs spread to Greece. The noted Greek physician Hippocrates (circa 460–375 B.C.E.) included in his writings roughly 400 herbal remedies. His remedies reflected his belief that all illnesses and diseases were caused by imbalances in the four bodily humors, which reflect nature's four elements: earth, water, fire, and air. When imbalances occurred, physicians recommended herbal remedies to restore harmony and facilitate healing. In ancient Britain, the Druidic priests, who were also healers, understood the planetary influences inherent in botanicals and used that knowledge when treating illness.

Plants grown naturally, without the assistance or interference of an outside source (such as a gardener or farmer), are referred to as "wildcrafted." Though cultivated herbs are grown in a controlled environment, they can be just as effective and potent as wild ones. You can purchase herbs fresh, dried, or in bulk from most greengrocers and farmers' markets. Note that a special relationship develops between the plants and the person who tends to them, so if you do not live in an area where you can find wild herbs, consider growing your own in a pot garden or window box.

When selecting botanicals, make sure they are full of vitality. Choose organic plants if possible. If you are purchasing your herbs and do not know under what conditions they were grown, make sure you wash them thoroughly to remove any residual chemicals that may have been used. You don't want the poisonous vibes of pesticides present in your spellwork! If you're harvesting a plant that you've grown or found in the wild, ask the plant's permission before harvesting it. Thank it for its help, whether you intend to eat it or use it in a spell. You might also choose to leave an offering in return for what you've received, such as a poured libation or a small crystal to honor the earth. You can also say "thanks" to the earth by cleaning up litter or other debris.

If you don't intend to use a plant immediately after harvesting it, dry it properly so that it will retain as much of its life force as possible. The best way to dry herbs is to hang them upside down in bunches in a cool, dry, relatively dark place. You can also dry them flat by spreading them out on a plate or cutting board wrapped in cloth. If you choose the flat drying method, you will need to turn the leaves, stems, or flowers frequently so that they dry evenly and do not rot.

You can either leave plants hanging in bunches or remove the leaves and flowers and store them in airtight jars or bottles made of dark glass (amber and cobalt). This slows the damaging effects of light and will preserve the herbs for a longer period of time.

Dandelion Blossom Oil

You can use this basic flower oil recipe for anointing candles and talismans. Dandelions grow wild and you may not prize them highly because they're "weeds," but their commonplace nature doesn't diminish their magickal power.

INGREDIENTS/TOOLS:

Dandelion blossoms

Jar with a tight lid

Cold-pressed olive oil or grape seed oil (amount determined by size of jar)

1 chopstick

Gather the dandelions at high noon on a sunny day—this imbues them with the radiant energy of the sun, and for practical purposes ensures that the blossoms will be dry. Fill your jar completely with the dandelion blossoms and pour in enough oil to completely fill the jar. Press out the air bubbles with the chopstick. Cap the jar and keep it in a cool, dry area. For the first two weeks, you'll need to open the jar every few days to press out the air bubbles and refill the jar with oil up to the top, making sure that the lid is tightly closed afterward. After that, you can use this lovely flower oil to anoint any objects you may use in your spellwork.

Using Botanicals in Magick

You can use botanicals, whether fresh or dried, in numerous ways. Put dried plant material in pouches to make amulets and talismans, or choose especially fragrant herbs and flowers for sachets and potpourri. Many of the spells in Part II use botanicals in this way.

Some plants may be burned in ritual fires, as offerings, or for purification. Sage is one of the most popular plants to use for this purpose. Many botanicals also come in the form of incense (sticks, cones, coils), which you can burn in spells and rituals—lots of the spells in Part II involve burning incense.

You can make an herbal infusion by boiling water, removing the water from the heat, and then adding herbs or flowers to the water. Let the plant material steep in the water for several minutes, and then strain and pour the water into a glass container. If you wish, set flowers in water and leave them in the sun to "steep." The essence of the flowers will be imparted to the water. Add a tiny amount of liquor such as brandy or vodka to the water to preserve it. Mist a room with flower water to purify it or sprinkle a little on an amulet or talisman to charge it.

You can prepare essential oils from plants if you like (although many people find it easier to purchase the oils). Oils are often used for anointing, consecrating, and blessing. You can add them to baths, too, and some may be ingested (but check first, as some are toxic). Each type of oil, like the plant from which it is derived, has its unique associations that enhance the power of your spell.

Burning a Ritual Fire

The Druids revered trees and understood the magickal nature of different types of trees. Oaks, for instance, symbolize strength and longevity; ashes and rowans provide protection; cedars attract prosperity; pines purify. You can burn a single type of wood or combine several in a ritual fire to produce a desired effect. If you decide to cut a twig or branch from a tree, remember to ask the tree's permission first and thank it afterward. Leaving an offering for the tree, such as some organic fertilizer, is also a nice idea.

THE POWER OF STONES

Long before people prized gems for monetary reasons, they valued stones for their magick properties. Spellworkers still do. You've probably already used gems for spells, although you may not have realized it at the time. Have you ever worn a piece of jewelry that contained your birthstone? Birthstones resonate with the energy of your zodiac sign and they've been worn since ancient times to enhance, modify, and balance a person's astrological makeup.

The dense nature of stones and their great endurance allows them to hold energy for a very long time. A gem that belonged to your great-grandmother probably still retains some of her energy resonance. This means that you can cast a spell using a stone and it will last for years. It also means that you need to cleanse stones before you work with them to remove any lingering vibes from people who handled them before you.

Just as each plant embodies certain characteristics and qualities that you can tap in spellwork, so does each stone. Often a stone's magickal properties relate to its color(s), perhaps even more than its mineral composition. Again, this is an example of sympathetic magick and the associations we place on colors. The following list shows the relationships between a stone's color and its magickal meaning:

- Red stones: Passion, courage, vitality
- Orange stones: Enthusiasm, good luck, self-confidence
- Yellow stones: Happiness, creativity (citrine or yellow quartz is used for cleansing)
- Green stones: Prosperity, growth, physical healing
- Blue stones: Peace, communication, psychic ability
- Purple stones: Wisdom, vision, connection with higher powers
- Pink stones: Love, friendship, social interactions, emotional balance
- White stones: Purity, cleansing, clarity, protection
- Black stones: Stability/permanence, banishing negativity, establishing boundaries

Gems are sacred in and of themselves, whether we choose to acknowledge them as such or not. They're not inert lumps; they possess life energy. That energy will manifest in your spells, so consider the gems you select and your connection with them carefully.

Preparing Stones for Spellwork

Amulets, talismans, and other types of spells frequently include stones. You may choose to use only one stone in a spell or combine several to fine-tune your objectives. Let's say, for example, that you're doing a love spell and you want to generate both passion and affection. In this case, you could incorporate both carnelian and rose quartz. If you seek stability too, add a piece of onyx.

If you only use one stone in your spellwork, let it be a clear quartz crystal. These readily available stones can do it all. They hold ideas and intentions; they attract and send information; they augment, focus, and direct energy; they store material for future use; they let you gaze into the future and the past. Crystals come in a variety of colors, due to minerals in their composition. Those colors provide clues to the crystals' use in spells.

Warning!

Don't drill holes in the stones you choose for your magick work. Gemstones and crystals are life forms, and if you bore into them or break them you may kill them. Instead, wrap them with wire or have a jeweler set them if you plan to wear them. Loose stones are great for amulets and talismans. Large stones aren't necessarily better than smaller ones—use your intuition and let yourself be drawn to the right stone for the job.

Before you begin working with gems and crystals, clear the stones of any residual energy left over from someone who may have previously handled the gems. Try one of the following methods:

- Wash the stone with mild soap and water, then leave it in the sunshine to dry. If you can hold it in the running water of a lovely, unpolluted stream, even better.
- Let the stone sit in the moonlight overnight to clear it.
- Smudge the gem by holding it in the smoke of burning sage or nestle it in a bed of dried sage leaves.
- Rub your stone gently with a piece of citrine (yellow quartz).
- Bury the gemstone in the earth for several days, or if possible, for the whole lunar month, beginning on the full moon.

Using Gemstones and Crystals in Spells

At the beginning of most chapters in Part II, you'll find a list of specific stones that witches and other magicians typically use for spells of certain types. Generally speaking, opaque stones work well in spells that involve material things; cloudy or translucent stones are best for emotional situations; clear stones relate to mental or spiritual conditions.

Crystals and gemstones are among a spellcaster's most basic and versatile tools. You can apply them in virtually any spell, in a variety of ways according to your preferences and the nature of the spell:

- Slip one or more stones and/or crystals into a mojo pouch or medicine bag to create a talisman or amulet.
- Carry a meaningful stone in your pocket to augment your personal energy.
- Wear gemstones/birthstones to heighten, calm, strengthen, balance, or otherwise influence your own energy patterns.
- Infuse water with a stone that relates to your intention, then remove the stone and drink the water.
- Add stones to bathwater to boost its healthful qualities.
- Place stones or crystals in your home to provide protection, harmonize energy patterns, or attract conditions you desire.
- Offer stones to deities and spirits in return for their assistance.
- Put a protection stone or quartz crystal in your car to keep you safe while traveling.
- Position stones on your body's chakras (energy centers) to promote health and well being (see Chapter 15).
- Gaze into a crystal to see beyond your normal range of vision; this is known as scrying.
- Use a gemstone or crystal as a pendulum to dowse (see Chapter 6).
- Meditate with stones and/or crystals to deepen your concentration and relaxation.
- Take a crystal with you when you travel and let it record the memory of the trip.
- Imprint a crystal with a message or intention, then direct it toward someone you wish to contact. You can do this by first holding the crystal to your forehead and sending your thoughts into the crystal, or by holding it to your lips and telling it what you want it to do. Then aim the crystal away from you and envision your message flowing out through the pointed end toward the other person.

This list barely scratches the surface of the magickal possibilities available to you. In Part II of this book, you'll find lots of spells that incorporate the power of gemstones and crystals. The more you work with stones, the more you'll discover. Treat your stones with love and respect. Cleanse them frequently to remove unwanted vibes (unless

The Modern Witchcraft Spell Book

they'll remain in place permanently as part of a spell). When you're not using them, store your stones in a safe place—wrapping them in silk will help to prevent ambient vibrations from affecting them. If you prefer, display them with pride on your altar or in another place of honor. Treat your crystals and gemstones as valued partners, and they will gladly work with you for a lifetime.

Chapter 5

THE POWER OF WORDS

Each of us is born with a wonderful instrument that we can use for healing, transformation, and magick: the voice. The earliest spells were probably spoken ones. Ancient shamans, witches, and sorcerers understood that sound and resonance had the power to shift reality. They may have uttered words that held meaning in an evident way, but that also contained sounds that impacted the ethers when said aloud. Today, spellworkers still use chants, prayers, affirmations, and other types of verbal magick, as you'll see when you get to Part II of this book.

In the mid-1990s, Japanese scientist Masaru Emoto began experimenting with how words affected water. He discovered that words could visibly alter the water's structure. Just as each snowflake is unique, Emoto found that each word produced a unique shape when the water was frozen. When the words *love, gratitude,* and *peace* were projected into the water, it froze into beautiful shapes. Expressions such as "I hate you" caused distorted, broken forms. The vibrational energy actually changed the physical appearance and the molecular shape of the water. Interestingly, it didn't matter what language was used. The words *love, amour, amore,* and the kanji symbol for love all generated similar snowflakes.

Because the universe—and everything in it—is composed of vibrations, all sounds produce effects. When you consider that all words create results, it makes sense to choose your words wisely and to think before you speak.

THE POWER OF PRAYER

For thousands of years, in cultures around the world, people have sought divine intervention to relieve suffering and attract blessings via the use of prayers. John Bunyan, a seventeenth-century English preacher and writer, said that prayer is the "sincere, sensible, affectionate pouring out of the soul to God." American poet Ralph Waldo Emerson described prayer as "a study of truth." The Unity Church calls prayer an "inward, silent knowing of the soul . . . of the presence of God." Witches view prayer as a means of communicating with the Divine.

Healing with Prayer

Like meditation, praying calms the mind and body, placing you in a gently altered state of consciousness where you can receive insights and guidance. On the physical level, blood pressure drops, heartbeat slows, breathing rate is lowered, and the adrenal glands secrete fewer of the stress-response hormones. Consequently, not only the recipient of the prayer benefits; so does the person who's praying. Prayer is also a demonstration of hope, and as you already know, hopefulness and a positive attitude can manifest beneficial results.

Whether you pray for yourself or someone else, your words have amazing power. According to Larry Dossey, MD, author of *Prayer Is Good Medicine*, in cases of intercessory prayer (praying for someone else at a distance) the consciousness of the person doing the praying actually influences the body of the person who is being prayed for. Dossey discovered that "more than 130 controlled laboratory studies show that prayer, or a prayerlike state of compassion, empathy and love, can bring about healthful changes." Numerous studies have shown that prayer can have a beneficial effect on a range of illnesses.

Prayer and Magick

Much of magickal work involves healing—doing spells for yourself or for others. Therefore, it's encouraging to realize that the results of your words and intentions can actually be measured scientifically. However, you can tap the power of prayer for virtually any purpose: to gain protection, to attract love, and so on.

When you pray to a higher power, it implies that you honor that higher power—God, Goddess, Spirit, your guardian angel, or however you envision it—and that an established relationship exists between you, which enables you to call on that higher power for aid. It also implies that you believe the higher power can remedy the situation. Prayer isn't begging or pleading with a deity to give you what you want—it's humbly aligning your personal will with Divine Will. You commit yourself to co-creating the best possible outcome, under the guidance of a higher power.

How to Pray

Prayer can take many forms, from the formal repetition in a church or temple of memorized verses taken from a religious text, to feeling grateful for a beautiful sunny day. You can pray silently or aloud, alone or with others, for yourself or someone else. You can pray first thing in the morning, before meals, at bedtime—or when you're stuck in traffic, in the shower, at your computer, or taking a walk in the park. You can even join an online prayer group. The Internet offers hundreds of sites where you can post a prayer request, respond to others who currently need help, or read the personal testimonies of people who believe they've been helped by prayers.

WORDS OF POWER

Spiritual and occult literature abounds with references to the power of the human voice. For millennia people have recited magick words as a way of evoking supernatural forces and petitioning them for assistance.

This is usually done by calling out the deities' names. Speaking someone's name is said to be an act of power, giving the namer influence over the named (which is why in some belief systems, individuals have "public" names and "private" names that are kept secret). In the Genesis story, Adam was allowed to name the animals on earth and thus was given dominion over them.

Witches and spellworkers recognize the power inherent in some words and use them in spells and rituals. You've undoubtedly heard the word *abracadabra*, but the word isn't just something a stage illusionist says before he pulls a rabbit out of a hat. It derives from the Aramaic *Avarah K'Davarah*, which translates to "I will create as I speak"; it expresses your intention to manifest a result. Ancient magicians wrote the word as an inverted pyramid and used it in healing spells. In Chapter 13, you'll learn how to do this, too.

Many witches end spells with the words "So mote it be." This phrase (like "So be it") seals a spell and instructs the universe to carry out your will. If you want to banish an entity or energy, you can order it to leave by saying, "Be gone." The expression "Blessed be" is a favorite greeting among witches and a magickal exchange of positive energy.

In spells, you can choose to speak or write a single word, a phrase, or a longer statement. Words such as *love, abundance, peace, happiness,* and *safety* instantly bring to mind the results you seek. When you say the words aloud, you send a ripple through the cosmos stating your intention. When you write the words, the acupressure points in your fingers trigger responses in your brain. Many of the spells in Part II use words as components.

I Am

One of the most powerful and sacred statements is also one of the shortest: I am. It connects you with your divine essence for creative purposes. You can consciously choose to form a sentence that begins with "I am" in order to manifest a desired condition. Be very careful how you use the phrase "I am." Whatever follows these words will be charged with magickal energy and intention. *Never* say hurtful or derogatory things such as "I am stupid" or "I am ugly"—these statements can materialize as unpleasant conditions.

The Modern Witchcraft Spell Book

AFFIRMATIONS

A good way to state your intention in a spell is to create what's called an affirmation. An affirmation is a short phrase or sentence that clearly and optimistically expresses whatever condition you desire to bring about. Affirmations leave no room for doubt, fear, or ambiguity. Whether you write affirmations or say them aloud, putting your intentions into words helps to focus your mind and empower your spells.

Creating Effective Affirmations

As is true with most things in life, there are "right" ways and "wrong" ways to design affirmations. These tips will help you to word yours effectively:

- Keep it short.
- Use only positive imagery.
- State your intention in the present tense, as if the condition already exists.

Let's try a couple examples to help you get a feel for designing affirmations.

Right: I am completely healthy in body, mind, and spirit.

Wrong: I don't have any illnesses or injuries.

See the difference? The first sentence affirms what you seek: health. The second makes you think of conditions you don't want: illnesses and injuries.

Right: I now have a job that's perfect for me.

Wrong: I will get the perfect job.

In the first sentence you state that the job you seek is yours right now. The second indicates that you'll eventually get the job you want, but it could be some time way off in the future.

Being specific is usually a good thing when creating affirmations. If your goal is to lose twenty-five pounds or you've got your heart set on acquiring a 1965 red Mustang convertible with black leather seats, for instance, list the pertinent details in your affirmation. But sometimes you don't know all the ins and outs of a situation, or you don't want to limit your options—as in the job example we just considered. Sometimes it's best to let the universe work out the fine points.

Here's a case in point. A friend of mine wanted to attract more money into her life, so she wrote this affirmation: "I now earn more than enough money for everything I need and desire." When I read what she'd written, I immediately noticed she'd limited her potential by using the word *earn*. I suggested she revise her affirmation so it said: "I now receive more than enough money for everything I need and desire." Soon afterward, she got an unexpected tax refund that fulfilled her affirmation.

Using Affirmations in Spells

When you cast a spell, you can say affirmations aloud if you like. Or you can write them on slips of paper and put them in mojo or medicine pouches, to use as talismans or amulets. Some people like to carve words into candles and then burn the candles during a spell. Another popular way to use affirmations is to write them on a vision board and place the board where you'll see it often. Each time you read the words, you'll be reminded of your objective. Once you understand the basics of creating affirmations, you'll probably find lots of original ways to include them in your spells and rituals.

INCANTATIONS

Want to kick an affirmation up a notch? Design it as an incantation. Incantations are written as rhymes. The catchy phrasing and rhythm make the incantation easy to remember. The rhythm also adds power to your statement by drawing upon nature's rhythmic patterns, e.g., waves breaking on the shore or the beat of your heart. Don't worry about the literary quality of your incantations; just follow the same guidelines for creating affirmations, then make your statements rhyme.

Incantations can be as short as two lines or as long as your imagination and intention dictate. You can use an incantation in the same way you'd use any other affirmation. Although it's perfectly okay to merely write an incantation, more often they are spoken aloud. Because incantations feature both rhyme and meter, you may enjoy putting them to music and singing them.

Here's an example of an incantation to attract love, from my book *Nice Spells/Naughty Spells*:

As the day fades into night
I draw a love that's good and right.
As the night turns into day
We are blessed in every way.

Okay, it's not going to win any awards for literary value, but it gets the message across and that's what counts. You'll find more incantations in Part II of this book. Creating incantations is fun—use your imagination to design your own. The more energy you infuse into your creation, the more effective it will be. If you do spellwork with other people, singing an incantation together raises the energy exponentially. Wiccans and witches often sing incantations at celebrations. Chanting a love incantation while dancing around a Maypole on Beltane, for instance, is a joyful and powerful form of magick.

CHANTS

When you think of chanting, your mind may produce an image of Buddhists uttering the Sanskrit phrase *Om Mani Padme Hum* or medieval monks intoning Gregorian chants in European cathedrals. Chants are typically phrases, words, or syllables repeated aloud for a particular purpose. Saying a rosary is a form of chanting, for example. Witches sometimes chant rhymes in their rituals to raise energy and to unify all the participants. Some shamans even use chanting to reconnect a person's soul with the physical body after a trauma has caused a separation.

Dr. Alfred Tomatis, a French eye, ear, and nose specialist affectionately known as "Dr. Mozart," noticed that the ear was the first sense organ to develop. According to Tomatis, frequencies in the range of 2,000 to 4,000 cycles per second—those found in the upper range of the human speaking voice—are the most beneficial in healing. These resonances stimulate vibrations in the cranial bones and the ear muscles, which then revitalize or "charge" the brain.

The repetitive nature of a chant, as well as the actual words that compose it, act on your subconscious to generate results. You may wish to accompany your chanting with drumming, clapping, rattles, dancing, or playing musical instruments, in order to increase psychic energy. The vibration of the chanting (as well as that of any other accompanying sound) has a measurable effect on the nervous system. At its height, chanting can even stimulate altered states of awareness, including ecstatic trances.

Some people chant mantras while meditating. A mantra is a group of sacred sounds repeated for spiritual purposes. The mantra not only helps you to focus, it lets you become aware of the spirit housed within your body. By recognizing this spirit and your connection with it, you move from the material world into the magickal realm. That's why it's often beneficial to meditate prior to doing spellwork.

You can chant to create circumstances you desire. You can also chant to enhance your link with divine entities or to call upon them for assistance. Chanting is a particularly good way to dispel unwanted energies. The cumulative power of the repeated sounds breaks down obstacles that might otherwise impede a spell's success, just as sound waves can break down obstructions such as kidney stones in the body.

SIGILS

Have you ever wanted to write in your own secret language? Guess what, you can. One way to do this is to design sigils to use in your spellwork. A sigil is a uniquely personal symbol you draw in order to produce a specific result. In a sense, a sigil is a way of communicating with yourself via secret code, because no one else can interpret the symbol. Although there are various techniques for designing sigils, the easiest one involves fashioning an image from letters.

Start by writing a word or a short affirmation that states your intention. Delete any letters that are repeated. For example, the word *SUC-CESS* contains three Ss and two Cs, but you only need to put one of each into your sigil. Entwine the remaining letters to form an image. You can use upper- and/or lower-case letters, block or script. Position them right-side up, upside down, forward, or backward. The end result depicts your objective in a graphic manner that your subconscious understands, although it won't make sense to anyone else. Each time you look at the sigil, you'll instantly recognize its meaning at a deep level and that reinforces your intention.

The following sigil takes the letters L O V E and combines them to create an image (the L is inherent to the E). Of course, you could configure the letters in a zillion different ways, according to your own preferences, and each design would be uniquely powerful. That's what makes sigils so special.

The process of creating the sigil as well as applying it are magick acts. Treat them that way. You may wish to design the sigil as a magickal working in itself and then use the sigil later as a component of another spell. In this way, you both craft and cast, and produce two effects by doing so: the crafting part—drawing the sigil—produces an effect on the person who draws it; it can then be used in casting another spell, for example the sigil for LOVE could be added to a love talisman. You can incorporate sigils into spells in myriad ways, for instance:

- Draw a sigil on a piece of paper and slip it into a mojo or medicine bag.
- Display a sigil on your altar to remind you of your intention.
- Hang one on the door to your home to provide protection.
- Carve one on a candle, and then burn the candle to activate your objective.
- Draw or embroider a sigil on a dream pillow.
- Add them to paintings, collages, or other artwork you create.

- Paint one on a glass so it can imprint water, wine, or another beverage with your intent.
- Have a jeweler fabricate your sigil as a pendant or pin and wear it as a talisman.
- Get a sigil tattooed on your body.

In Part II of this book, you'll find suggestions for using sigils in spells. There's no limit to how many sigils you can draw or how many ways you can use them. Give your imagination free rein.

Chapter 6

MAGICK TOOLS AND ACCOUTREMENTS

Carpenters use hammers, saws, screwdrivers, and lots of other tools in their work. Chefs use knives, spoons, bowls, pots, and pans. What do spellworkers use? Technically speaking, you don't need anything except your mind to cast a spell. However, people who do magick generally use certain tools and accoutrements, in part because these help you to focus and therefore achieve greater success with your spells.

The tools you use to do magick speak to your subconscious mind. A tool's shape, material, and other features provide clues to its symbolism and thus its role in spellwork, according to the concept of sympathetic magick. Although some items may look familiar, their magickal purposes may differ significantly from their roles in the mundane world. In this chapter, we'll look at some of the most popular tools witches, wizards, and other spellworkers use and the roles these implements play in spells. Remember, however, that even the most elegant tool requires your will to empower it. You may decide to work with a few of these, all, or none—it's up to you entirely.

Masculine and Feminine Energies

When we speak of masculine and feminine energies, we don't mean man and woman. Instead, we're referring to the complementary forces that exist everywhere in our universe: action (masculine) and receptivity (feminine). You'll notice that a spellcaster's tools correspond to the human body, symbolically depicting those energies. The wand and the athame, which represent masculine power, look distinctly phallic. The chalice and cauldron signify feminine energy and the womb. The five rays of the pentagram stand for the five "points" of the body: the head, arms, and legs.

THE WAND

You're familiar with magick wands, no doubt. The fairy tales we loved as children told us that you could tap a guy on the head with a magick wand and turn him into a frog or make him disappear. That's not the reason spellworkers use wands, though. A wand's real purpose is to direct energy. You can either attract or send energy with your wand. Aim it at the heavens to draw down cosmic power. Point it toward a person, place, or thing to project energy toward your goal. Some magicians cast circles with their wands.

Choosing Your Wand

What material makes the best wand? Traditionally, magicians used wood for their wands, particularly willow, yew, hazel, or rowan. But you don't have to hold with tradition. If you prefer, select a wand fabricated from metal, glass, quartz, ceramic—whatever "calls" to you. If you decide you want a wooden wand and plan to cut a small branch from a tree, always ask the tree's permission first and thank it when you've finished. (It's nice to give the tree an offering in return, too.) Cutting a wand is a ritual in itself, so approach the task with the proper mindset.

Your wand should be at least six inches long, but no longer or heavier than you find comfortable to handle. Are you a down-to-basics kind of person? If so, you might want to leave your wand in its natural state. Would you enjoy something more ornate? Then decorate your wand to suit your fancy. Again, the choice is yours; however, because the wand is considered a "fire" tool, you might like to enhance its fiery nature with appropriate adornments, such as:

- Red, orange, or gold paint
- Gold, brass, or iron accents
- Red or orange gemstones: garnet, ruby, carnelian, red jasper
- Astrological glyphs for the fire signs: Aries, Leo, Sagittarius
- Red or orange ribbons, feathers, beadwork, etc.

Charging Your Wand

Now it's time to infuse your wand with magickal power. This transforms it from a stick of wood or a metal rod into an awesome tool for spellwork. Witches, wizards, and other magicians often enact a ritual or ceremony to charge their tools. It can be as simple or elaborate as you wish; your intention and attitude are the most important factors. Part of my wand-charging ritual involved hanging my wand from a tree in the sunshine for a solar month. Because charging your wand is a magickal act, approach the ritual with the proper mindset and perform it within a circle.

You might consider one or more of the following techniques:

- Hold your wand in the smoke of a ritual fire.
- Anoint it with essential oil(s): cinnamon, sandalwood, clove, musk.
- Carve it with words and/or symbols of power.
- Chant an incantation you've composed for this purpose.
- Play energizing music.

Clearly and authoritatively instruct your wand to do your bidding. Command it to work with you and only you. Point it toward the south and invite the energy of fire to enter it. Breathe your own energy into the wand to bring it to life. When you've finished, state aloud: So mote it be!

These suggestions are just that: suggestions. The best and most powerful charging rituals are those you design yourself. Put lots of energy and enthusiasm into your work. Pull out all the stops. Make it as personal as you can—the more meaningful it is to you, the better.

PENTAGRAM

The pentagram is a five-pointed star with a circle around it. Many witches wear this symbol for protection. You might choose to display one on the door to your home or place of business as a safeguard. Keep a pentagram in your car and on your altar. Draw them on paper and slip them into mojo or medicine pouches to make amulets. Carve pentagrams into candles and burn them during spellwork. In circle casting, you can trace pentagrams in the air or on the ground at the four directions to ensure safety. Many of the protection spells in Chapter 11 use pentagrams.

Choosing a Pentagram

The pentagram represents the earth element and is linked with the feminine force. Consequently, you might like to have a pentagram made of silver (a metal ruled by the moon) or copper (which is ruled by Venus). Perhaps you'd like to decorate your pentagram with crystals or gemstones, especially if you plan to wear it as a piece of jewelry. No material is inherently right or wrong, better or worse—it really depends on how you intend to use your pentagram.

Although you will probably only use one magick wand, you can have as many pentagrams as you want. You might like one made of ceramic, glass, or wood on which to serve food during rituals, perhaps decorated with the astrological glyphs for the earth signs: Taurus, Virgo, and Capricorn. If you're handy, you can embroider pentagrams on ritual clothing. If you plan to hang a pentagram outside, make sure it can withstand weather conditions. Display your pentagram with one point up, two down, and two out at the sides.

Charging Your Pentagram

As discussed earlier, the ritual of charging your tools empowers them and transforms them into magickal instruments. Consider the act of charging your pentagram a spell, and do it with the appropriate intent. You may choose to create an intricate ritual to charge it, or keep it simple. Here are a few suggestions:

- Mist it with flower water made with carnation, snapdragon, geranium, and/or hyacinth petals. (If your pentagram is made of metal, pat it dry to prevent tarnishing.)
- Anoint it with essential oil(s): amber, basil, pine, fennel.
- Bury it in the earth for a period of time, perhaps a week. (You may need to encase it in a protective container.)
- Lay it on your altar and place crystals at each of the five points and in the center.
- Chant an incantation you've composed for this purpose.
- Let it sit in the moonlight overnight.

Clearly and authoritatively instruct your pentagram to do your bidding. Command it to work with you and only you. Point it toward the north and invite the energy of earth to enter it. Breathe your own energy into the pentagram to bring it to life. When you've finished, state aloud: So mote it be!

ATHAME

The origins of the word *athame* have been lost to history. Some people speculate that it may have come from *The Key of Solomon* (*Clavicula Salomonis*) (published in 1572), which refers to the knife as the *Arthana* (*athame* may be a subverted form of this term). Another theory proposes that *athame* derives from the Arabic word *al-dhamme* (blood-letter), a sacred knife in the Moorish tradition. In either case, manuscripts dating back to the 1200s imply the use of ritual knives in magick work.

The athame's main purpose is to symbolically clear negative energies from a space you'll use in spellworking. You can also slice through obstacles or sever bonds with it, again symbolically. It needn't be sharp—you won't be chopping veggies with it. Some Wiccans and witches like to cast a circle with an athame instead of a wand.

Choosing Your Athame

This ritual dagger is usually a double-edged knife about four to six inches long. Some Wiccans, however, prefer crescent-shaped athames that represent the moon. Most athames are made of metal, but yours can be crystal, glass, or another material. An ordinary kitchen knife will work, too. If you like something more elegant, choose one that's adorned with crystals or gemstones. Because this tool symbolizes the air element, consider stones associated with air, such as aquamarine, fluorite, or clear quartz.

If you decide to purchase a vintage dagger for your magick work, make sure it hasn't drawn blood in the past. Some magicians believe that an athame used to physically harm another will never again be functional in magick, although in ancient times witches often "fed" special knives by rubbing them with blood.

Charging Your Athame

Before you use your athame in spellwork, charge it to make it truly "yours" and to imbue it with magickal power. Remember, this is a spell in itself, so approach the process accordingly. How you go about charging your athame is up to you—you can simply command it to do your will, or design a ritual with all sorts of bells and whistles. Here are some possibilities:

- Hold it in the smoke of burning incense.
- Anoint it with essential oil(s): carnation, lavender, ginger.
- Attach feathers to its hilt and/or decorate the hilt with the astrological glyphs for the air signs: Gemini, Libra, or Aquarius.

- Tie yellow or light blue ribbons on it, and recite a prayer or incantation with each knot.
- Play flute music, ring a bell, or place your athame near wind chimes to receive their sounds.

Clearly and authoritatively instruct your athame to do your bidding. Command it to work with you and only you. Point it toward the east and invite the energy of air to enter it. Breathe your own energy into the athame to bring it to life. When you've finished, state aloud: So mote it be!

CHALICE

The fourth major tool in the witch's tool kit is the chalice, which symbolizes the element of water. During rituals and rites, witches often drink ceremonial beverages from a chalice—many chalices feature long stems so they can be passed easily from hand to hand. Sharing the cup with coven members or spellworkers signifies connectedness and unity of purpose. You may choose to drink magick potions you've concocted from your chalice. Spellworkers also serve magickal elixirs, for healing or other purposes, in a special chalice.

The most famous chalice of all is the Holy Grail. The Grail myths embody far more information than we can go into here, but you may wish to examine them to gain a greater understanding of the magickal meaning of the chalice. Shaped like the womb, the chalice represents feminine fertility, power, and creativity in the larger sense. This potent vessel holds the waters of life and nurtures the imagination that births all things in the manifest world.

Choosing Your Chalice

Your chalice is a sacred vessel from which you will sip magick potions and ceremonial beverages. As such, it should be reserved for these special occasions—don't drink Coke from it at lunchtime. Depending on your preferences, your chalice may be simple or ornate. Some people choose chalices made of silver, because silver is a metal ruled by the moon and the chalice is a feminine tool. Others prefer crystal, colored glass, or ceramic chalices—the choice is entirely yours. You could even use an ordinary water glass or coffee cup, but that might not be quite as much fun. The beauty of the chalice, the way it feels in your hand, and the sound it makes when you clink it to another chalice in a toast all contribute to the experience.

In Chapter 5, we talked about Japanese scientist Masaru Emoto's work with imprinting water with words. Because the liquids that go into your chalice will absorb the energy of whatever images are on the vessel, it's best to choose a plain chalice without pictures, words, or patterns, as those may affect your spells. If you wish, you can decorate your chalice with temporary images that relate to your intentions for a spell and remove those images when you've finished.

Charging Your Chalice

Until you charge your chalice, it's just an ordinary vessel. Once you've imbued it with your magickal energy, it becomes your own "Grail." The ritual you enact to charge your chalice may be simple or complex, depending on your preferences. I charged my chalice by submerging it in a sacred pool for a lunar month. Because this tool symbolizes the element of water, many magicians choose to charge it with water or another liquid. Here are some suggestions:

- Spritz it with flower water made from jasmine, rose, lotus, or gardenia blossoms.
- Sprinkle it with "holy" water from a well, spring, or lake that holds special meaning for you. (Pat metal chalices dry afterward to prevent tarnishing.)
- Nestle the chalice in a bed of white rose petals, and leave it overnight.
- Anoint it on the outside with essential oil(s): rose, jasmine, ylang-ylang, gardenia.
- Paint your chalice with the astrological glyphs for Cancer, Scorpio, or Pisces.
- Place a piece of rose quartz, amethyst, moonstone, or a pearl in the chalice and fill it with spring water. Let it sit overnight, then remove the gem and either drink the water or pour it into a clear glass jar for use later.

- Play a singing bowl near your chalice to infuse it with positive vibrations. Singing bowls are usually made of metal or crystal and they have different musical tones. You strike them or run a mallet around the rim to create sound, which can be used for meditation, healing, or other purposes.

Clearly and authoritatively instruct your chalice to do your bidding. Command it to work with you and only you. Hold it so that the bowl of the chalice faces west and invite the energy of water to enter it. Breathe your own energy into the chalice to bring it to life. When you've finished, state aloud: So mote it be!

Magick Tools and the Tarot

You can see these four main tools illustrated in the beautiful oracle known as the tarot (which we'll talk about later). Each suit in the deck of cards is named for one of these tools: wands (sometimes called rods or staves), swords (or daggers, meaning athames), cups (or chalices), and pentacles (or pentagrams, sometimes called coins or disks). As such, they describe fundamental life energies and ways of interacting with the world.

CANDLES

The most common and versatile tool you're likely to use in your magickal practice, candles play a role in lots of rituals and spells. They also brighten many of our secular and religious celebrations. The concept of illumination carries both a practical meaning—visible light that enables you to see to conduct your daily tasks—and an esoteric one—an inspiration or awakening that enlivens mundane existence and expands understanding. The flame represents the element of fire, inspiration, clarity, passion, activity, energy, and purification. It can also signify Spirit.

You can use candles to set the stage for magick; their soft, flickering glow transports the spellworker into another level of awareness. You can gaze into a candle's flame to see beyond the ordinary limits of vision, even into the past or future. Many witches and other magicians use candles to tap color relationships in spellwork—burning a candle of a relevant color can augment a spell or ritual. "Dressing" or anointing your candles with essential oils adds another sensory dimension. As you evolve in your work as a spellcaster, you'll probably want to stock up on candles in various colors, sizes, and shapes—tapers for creating moods, pillars for long-term spells, votives for shorter spells/rituals and circle casting, and so on.

Some witches like to make their own candles, blending the wax with herbs/flowers, essential oils, and dyes that represent their intentions. You can even form candle wax into shapes that signify your objectives. In Part II, you'll find lots of spells that use candles in various ways to produce magickal results.

INCENSE

For thousands of years, aromatic gums and resins have been used in sacred rituals. Ancient Chinese and Indian texts describe the therapeutic, philosophical, and spiritual properties of aromatics. Churches and temples use incense to clear the air and to honor deities. In Buddhist belief, burning an offering of incense invites the Buddha into a statue of the holy being. Incense also serves as a vehicle for conveying prayers to the spirit world—as the smoke rises, it carries your requests along with it.

Aromas trigger instantaneous reactions in the brain. Inhaling certain smells can cause measurable responses involving memory, emotions, awareness, and more. That's one reason magickal workers include scents in their spells.

Burning incense combines the elements of fire and air. You can use it to cast a circle by walking the perimeter and trailing the fragrant smoke behind you. For balance, walk the circle a second time while sprinkling saltwater to represent the elements of earth and water. You can also charge talismans, amulets, and other magickal tools with incense by holding them in the smoke for a few moments.

Many witches purify a sacred space with incense. Sage is the most frequently used herb for this purpose, but you can burn pine, frankincense, sandalwood, eucalyptus, or another scent if you prefer. The best incense is blended from pure gums and resins, without synthetic binders.

You can even make your own by grinding up aromatic wood or resin (with a mortar and pestle or a coffee grinder) and adding finely powdered herbs or dried flowers.

Choose a scent that matches your intentions. You'll find lists at the beginnings of most chapters in Part II that show which scents correspond to love, money, protection, and so on.

Essential Oils

Like incense, aromatic oils enhance your sensory experience during a spell or ritual. These plant extracts contain the life energy of the plant, its unique signature and "soul essence." Unlike commercial fragrances, they do not include synthetic ingredients in their composition. You can use essential oils to dress candles, anoint talismans and amulets, charge magick tools, add to ritual baths, perfume your skin, and lots more. Use caution, however, because some oils can cause allergic reactions and some are toxic if ingested. Because essential oils are volatile, store them in a cool, dark place to prevent deterioration.

CAULDRON

According to Norse mythology, the god Odin received wisdom and the gift of intuition from a cauldron. Celtic legend mentions a cauldron as a tool of regeneration for the gods, and artists often depict the Irish creativity goddess Brigid stirring a cauldron. Stories such as these give us clues to the symbolic value of the cauldron today. Its shape represents the womb from which all life flows and its three legs represent the threefold nature of human existence: body, mind, spirit.

The cauldron performs both symbolic and practical functions. You can use a cauldron to cook ritual foods and to concoct magick potions. It also serves as a handy vessel for holding water, flowers, or other items at a ceremony or ritual. If you like, you can build a fire inside your cauldron and drop wishes written on paper into the flames—the cauldron's creative qualities nurture your requests and bring them to fruition. Build your fire of sacred woods that pertain to your purpose: cedar for prosperity, ash for protection, apple for love. Although usually iron, a cauldron can be made of any fireproof material including copper, steel, or terra cotta—you can even draft an ordinary cooking pot into duty if need be.

SPELL BOTTLES

Spell or "witch" bottles contain items with similar energies, brought together for a specific intention. Depending on your purpose, the bottle can be a temporary or permanent fixture. Select a glass bottle that's large enough to hold all the ingredients you plan to put in it, then wash and dry it to remove any unwanted energies. Make sure all the ingredients correspond to your objective. Add botanicals, gemstones, coins, milagros, shells, or anything else that symbolizes your intention. You may wish to write an affirmation or sigil on a slip of paper, roll the paper into a scroll, and then put it into the bottle, too.

When you're certain you've included everything you need for your spell, close the lid and seal the bottle with wax dripped from a candle that you've designated as part of the spell. Once the spell is cast, the bottle should remain sealed. You may choose to place your mark on the wax seal and/or decorate the outside of the bottle with symbols, words, images, ribbons, etc. that relate to your spell. Place the bottle on your altar or in another spot in your home or business, depending on its purpose. If you prefer, bury the bottle in a special place. Spell bottles also make great gifts—personalize them with good wishes for friends who won't think you're too weird.

OTHER TOOLS AND ACCOUTREMENTS

What else might you want to put into your magick chest? Anything that you feel adds to your craft as a spellcaster. If wearing elegant ritual clothing enhances your sense of power or makes you feel part of another dimension, by all means dress up. If music elevates your mood or takes you into another place emotionally, play your favorite CDs or an instrument, if you have musical talent.

Oracles

Divination is the art of predicting the future. The word literally means to "let the divine realm manifest." An oracle may be a person with special abilities to see beyond the limits of the visible world—a psychic, astrologer, or shaman. Physical tools such as tarot cards and runes are also called oracles; magick workers consult them to gain guidance and advice. You can also use them in spells, as you'll see when you get to Part II of this book:

- Tarot—As mentioned earlier, these beautiful cards typically contain four suits that correspond to the four major tools we talked about at the beginning of this chapter. Each of the seventy-eight cards in a tarot deck has a special meaning based on its suit, number, colors, and many other things. You can lay out patterns of cards known as "spreads" for divination purposes, or you can use a single card in a spell. (My books *The Everything® Tarot Book* and *The Only Tarot Book You'll Ever Need* offer in-depth information about the meanings of the cards and instructions for using them.)
- Runes—The word *rune* means "secret" or "mystery." Most people think of the early Norse alphabet when they hear "runes." If you're a fan of J.R.R. Tolkien's books, you've already heard about runes. The most popular alphabet contains twenty-four letters, and each letter is named for an animal, object, condition, or deity. They also convey deeper meanings that you can tap in spellwork, as you'll soon see. You might also enjoy working with Ogham runes. These twenty letters from the old Celtic alphabet correspond to different trees, and like Norse runes they hold secret meanings. The letters are composed of lines, or notches, cut along a central line or stave. A phrase written in Ogham looks like a tree limb with branches sprouting from it. You can cast runes made of wood, stone, ceramic, etc. for divination purposes, or choose individual runes for spellwork.
- Pendulum—A pendulum usually consists of a small weight, such as a crystal, hung from a short chain or cord. You hold the chain, letting the pendulum dangle at the end of it, while you ask a simple question. The pendulum's movement—back and forth, side to side, around and around—has meaning and answers your question. The

pendulum swings of its own accord—you don't influence its movement. When you use a pendulum, you're doing a form of dowsing. Most people think of dowsing as searching for water hidden underground, but that's only one method. When you consult a pendulum for the purpose of divination, you're searching for answers hidden deep within yourself.

Ribbons and Ropes

I'm a big fan of knot magick, and I've recommended using ribbons and ropes in many of the spells in Part II. When you tie a knot, you capture the mental and emotional energy present at the time in the knot and hold that energy there until you're ready to use it. Ancient mariners tied the wind into knots; if they were becalmed at sea, they opened the knots to release the wind and continued on their way.

You can also use ribbons to secure mojo pouches and medicine bags, so your magick stays inside. You'll find spells in Part II that use this method. Magick cords can also tie people together in a personal or professional relationship. If you believe an enemy is trying to harm you, you can bind that person or spirit by symbolically tying up him, her, or it with rope. A quick study of numerology will reveal the significance of numbers in spellworking and help you determine how many knots you'll need to tie in order to support your intentions: two for love, four for security, etc.

Make a Joyful Noise

Drums and rattles serve various purposes in magickal work. They raise energy. They break up blockages and stimulate sluggish conditions. They send messages far and wide. They can induce trances. They unify the minds and emotions of a group of people who choose to work together. They connect you with the spirit realm, and much more.

Bells can signal steps in a ritual. Bells and wind chimes also disperse unwanted energies and inspire harmony. Singing bowls help to balance the body's energy centers (chakras). They also calm and focus your mind, and connect you with higher levels of being.

Keep a Record

A grimoire or book of shadows is a witch's collection of magick recipes, spells, charms, invocations, and rituals. Here's where you keep a record of the magick you perform, the ingredients and tools you use, the potions, formulae, and incantations you create—and, of course, the results you generate. It's also a good idea to date each entry and note whatever else you consider significant, such as the moon's phase, your feelings, and anyone who participated in the spell/ritual with you. Many people prefer physical books for this purpose—the more ornate the better—but you can keep a computer version of a grimoire if you choose. You might want to take a look online at some of the beautiful old grimoires from medieval Europe, and even as far back as ancient Babylonia.

Pretty much anything can become a magickal instrument if you deem it so. Use what you consider necessary and what feels right to you. Over time, you may wish to add other tools to your collection or to devise your own. Remember to treat your tools with respect. When not in use, place them in a safe spot where they won't get damaged or handled by other people. You may wish to wrap them in silk or store them in a pretty box to protect them from ambient vibrations, as well as ordinary dust and dirt. With proper care, they should last a long time and serve you well.

Chapter 7

SPELLWORKING WITH SPIRITS

Do you believe in angels? Ghosts? Other spirit beings? If so, you're not alone. Throughout history, people have believed in nonphysical entities of many kinds. The ancient Greek, Roman, and Egyptian pantheons, for example, included lots of gods, goddesses, and lesser deities who performed a variety of tasks in this world and beyond. The Celts, Norse, Chinese, Hindi, and Native Americans all looked to divine beings for guidance and aid. Christianity honors an assortment of saints, and many traditions speak of angels. Our ancestors even credited spirits with bringing about natural occurrences, such as lightning and floods, and wove intricate myths around these supernatural beings.

We've already talked a little about spellworking with spirits and how they can help you in your magickal practice. In fact, spirits may be giving you a hand even if you don't realize it or haven't specifically asked for their assistance. What do we mean by spirits? In a very general sense, for the purposes of this book, we're referring to nonphysical beings who exist in another level of reality and with whom you can interact in some way. That's a broad and overly simplistic definition, and it includes many more entities than we'll discuss here. Gods and goddesses, angels, guides and guardians, ancestors, elementals, spirit animals, fairies, nature spirits, friends and loved ones who've left the material world, and many more may connect with you from time to time across "the Great Divide." In some cases, you can call upon them to assist you in spellworking.

Magick Cats

The ancient Egyptians revered cats as deities, but the Celts also attributed supernatural powers to felines. In Irish folklore, cat sidhe (otherworldly beings) guard access to the Underworld and its treasure. Magick white cats accompany the Welsh goddess Ceridwin. Images of cats appear on special stones in Scotland, put there by an ancient race known as the Picts. Female fairies and witches have long been known to keep cats as familiars (magickal companions) and to shapeshift into cats.

GODS AND GODDESSES

Do you feel an affinity with a particular culture, race, religion, or nation? If so, you may wish to study those people and their gods and goddesses. If you feel drawn to ancient Egypt, for instance, you might want to learn more about Isis, Bast, Hathor, Osiris, or Thoth. If you're Irish, you may sense a connection with Brigid, Ceridwin, or Lugh. But you needn't look only to deities with whom you share some lineage or common ground.

The Right God/dess for the Job

My previous books, *The Modern Guide to Witchcraft* and *The Everything® Wicca and Witchcraft Book*, contain lists of gods and goddesses from various cultures, along with their attributes. If you plan to call upon deities for assistance in spellwork, look to those whose characteristics and special powers relate to your intention(s). For example:

- In love spells, seek aid from Venus, Aphrodite, Freya, or Aengus.

- For prosperity spells, call upon Lakshmi, Zeus, or the Green Man (a pagan woodland deity, associated with fertility and popular in Celtic mythology).
- Ask Brigid, Ceres, or Lugh for assistance with healing spells.
- If you seek protection, call on Artemis, Tara, or Horus.
- To gain wisdom or inspiration, ask Brigid, Ceridwin, Sophia, Mercury, Odin, or Thoth for help.
- Spells for courage or strength could benefit from the help of Mars, Sekhmet, or Ganesh.

Sometimes all you have to do to enlist a deity's aid is ask. However, you can show your sincerity by placing an image of the god or goddess on your altar, or in another place of honor. If the deity has a holiday associated with him or her, celebrate it. You can also make an offering to a deity—incense, flowers, gemstones, etc. Do a little research to see if the god/dess you wish to contact has a favorite.

Calling a God or Goddess

After you've determined which deity you want to work with, cast a circle and invite that god/dess to join you in your sacred space. You can do this alone or with a group. You may wish to devote your altar to the deity for the term of the spell, or longer. Light a candle and incense, if you like, to help transport you mentally into another level of reality.

1. Clear your mind, center yourself, feel your connection to the earth and the heavens.
2. Allow your intuition and your personal energy to expand, becoming lighter and more sensitive.
3. Hold your arms out to your side, palms open, as if to embrace the deity whose presence you seek.
4. Call to the deity by name and request that he or she join you. This petition can be as simple or as eloquent as you choose. Some people invite the deity into their own bodies, but that's not necessary in most instances and involves a bit more skill.
5. When you sense the presence of the god/dess, continue with whatever magick you've chosen to perform.

If you're working outdoors, the deity may manifest through a sign or natural occurrence, such as a clap of thunder if the day is stormy, the parting of clouds, an increase in the wind, or other such phenomena. Sometimes the token spirit animal associated with the deity appears—e.g., a deer if you've called upon Diana. Sometimes the god/dess will speak directly in the form of an oracle. Often you simply feel a heightened sense of energy, awareness, or power, and you know the deity is there with you.

After you've finished your spellwork, release the deity. Many people like to compose a poetic parting statement, but you can say something as simple as: "Thank you [NAME] for your assistance here today. May you return home safely, and may there be peace between us." Remember to show respect and gratitude, just as you would if a human being had given you assistance in your pursuit. Then open the circle, trusting that with the deity's aid your spell will succeed.

SPIRIT ANIMALS

In ancient times, people in many parts of the world believed spirit animals lived in an invisible realm that intersects with our own physical one. These spirit beings helped our ancestors in countless ways, from providing food and protection to offering healing wisdom to predicting the future. Early humans considered these animal guides and guardians as deities—somewhat like angels—and paid homage to them.

What Are Spirit Animals?

Some traditions say that animal guides once lived on earth as physical creatures and passed over into the spirit world after death. Other views suggest that spirit beings never actually existed in the flesh—although their earthly counterparts may embody the spirits' energies. Still others tell us that spirit animals can assume the forms of physical creatures when they want to and can move between the worlds of ordinary and non-ordinary reality at will. People who study and work with spirit animals generally agree on one thing, however: These entities willingly offer us their help, and you can tap their special powers to enhance your well-being.

You've probably heard of "totems." The term refers to an animal, bird, reptile, fish, or insect with which you feel a strong and perhaps inexplicable affinity. A totem is your primary spirit animal guardian, or the guardian of your family or group. That being is always with you, protecting and guiding you. However, your personal totem may invite other animals to assist on occasions when you need a little extra help or when you're facing a challenge that requires the special characteristics of another creature.

Working with Spirit Animals

Ask your primary animal guide to make itself known to you. Try not to hold any expectations about what creature will appear. Perhaps you'll see a vision of it in your mind's eye or sense its presence near you. It might show up in a dream, or you may encounter its physical counterpart in nature. Trust that it will appear when the time is right and that the experience will be a positive one.

Showing respect and admiration for your totem animal is an essential part of working with it. This creature has a great deal to offer you, so you'll want to express gratitude. You can do this in a variety of ways:

- Find pictures of your totem in magazines or online and display them in your home or workplace.
- Learn as much as you can about your animal.
- Draw, paint, or sculpt images of your totem.
- Write a poem or story about your spirit animal.
- Watch animal shows on TV.
- Wear jewelry or clothing with the animal's picture on it.
- Go to a park, beach, farm, wildlife sanctuary, zoo, or other place to see your totem in the flesh.
- Join an animal welfare organization.
- Give money to a charity that protects animals and/or their habitat.

Once you've established a close relationship with your spirit animal guide or guides, you can ask them to assist you in all sorts of magickal work. Spirit animals can teach you their unique skills, provide protection, aid in healing, carry messages to and from other worlds, and do much more. My book *The Secret Power of Spirit Animals* contains lots of information about these amazing beings and how to work with them.

Familiars, Totems, and Pets

The term *familiar* refers to a special animal, bird, or other creature that works with a person to produce magickal results. Remember Harry Potter's owl? A familiar's physical and spiritual qualities can help you in spellworking. Sometimes a beloved pet might be a familiar, but that's not always the case. Your totem might share its powers through a familiar, but your totem doesn't necessarily serve as your familiar, nor is your familiar necessarily your totem.

ANGELS

In 2011, a poll conducted by the Associated Press found that 77 percent of Americans believe in angels. Many people report having received help from angels, especially during times of crisis or in periods of hopelessness and despair. According to some sources, everyone has a personal guardian angel who hears your prayers, watches over you, and helps you handle the challenges in your life.

Angelic Hierarchies

In some traditions, a hierarchy of angelic forces exists, with many ethereal beings at ascending levels of power. The Old Testament of the Bible lists them in the following order, from the lowest to the highest:

Level 1: Personal guardian angels

Level 2: Archangels

Level 3: Principalities (Princes)

Level 4: Powers

Level 5: Virtues

Level 6: Dominions

Level 7: Thrones (Orphanim)

Level 8: Cherubim

Level 9: Seraphim

Connecting with Your Guardian Angel

Do you sense the presence of your own guardian angel? If not, you may want to try one or more of the following:

- Before falling asleep, ask your angel to appear to you in a dream.
- Light incense and send your request to your angel in the rising smoke.
- On a slip of paper write a message to your angel, fold it three times, then burn it in your cauldron, fireplace, barbecue grill, or other safe spot.
- Place a figurine or picture of an angel on your altar.
- Meditate and listen for your angel's "voice."
- Observe nature. You might see your angel in the clouds, a body of water, a flower, or elsewhere.

Spellworking with Angels

Magick workers often invite angels to participate in rituals, both to provide protection and to augment the powers of the people involved in the ritual. Usually the angel Raphael is associated with the east, Michael with the south, Gabriel with the west, and Uriel with the north. You can use the following circle casting technique to invite these angelic beings to join you in your spellwork or ritual. Feel free to elaborate on this basic formula—make it as evocative as you like. Use your imagination.

1. Face east and hold your wand outstretched before you. Say aloud: "Angel Raphael, guardian of the east, be here now."
2. Turn clockwise and face south. Hold your wand outstretched before you. Say aloud: "Angel Michael, guardian of the south, be here now."
3. Turn clockwise and face west. Hold your wand outstretched before you. Say aloud: "Angel Gabriel, guardian of the west, be here now."
4. Turn clockwise and face north. Hold your wand outstretched before you. Say aloud: "Angel Uriel, guardian of the north, be here now."
5. Turn clockwise again until you reach the point at which you started to complete the circle, then proceed with your spell.

At the end of the spell or ritual, release the angels you've called in and thank them for assisting you. Again, you can use a simple, straight-forward statement or a more colorful one that you create yourself. Open the circle in reverse order from how you cast it.

ELEMENTALS

Elementals are so named because they represent the four elements: earth, air, fire, and water. Most of the time you can't see them, though occasionally they cross over into our range of vision. They often figure prominently in folklore, fairy tales, and legends. If you befriend them, elementals can serve as devoted helpers who will eagerly assist you in performing magick spells.

However, these capricious beings aren't above playing tricks on you—especially if they feel you've dissed them or they just don't like you. Treat elementals with consideration, respect, and a bit of caution. Always remember to thank the elementals who assist you in your spellworking, too, and perhaps offer them a small gift to show your appreciation.

Gnomes

Gnomes are earth spirits. Sometimes called trolls, elves, or lepre-chauns, these elementals are practical, no-nonsense creatures that may appear a bit gruff. However, they possess a wonderful appreciation for material things and can be valuable aides when you're doing prosperity spells. They can also assist you with practical and mundane matters. Gnomes enjoy a bit of bling, so give them a piece of jewelry, a pretty crystal, or a few shiny coins to thank them for their help.

Sylphs

What people often think of as fairies are most likely air spirits, known as sylphs. They often look like tiny lights or flickering sparks. Because their specialty is communication, they can help you with negotiating contracts, writing term papers, pitching ideas, or other matters that involve communication. Sylphs naturally gravitate to intelligent, liter-ary, and analytical people. They're especially fond of flowers, so place fresh blossoms on your altar or lay them in a sacred spot outdoors as an offering.

Salamanders

No, I don't mean lizards. These are the fire spirits, lively entities who are naturally drawn to people who exhibit creativity and initiative. When you do spells that involve action, inspiration, daring, or passion, salamanders can serve as liaisons, marshaling the forces of the fire realm to assist you. Call on them when you need an infusion of courage or vitality; they can also help you initiate a project or embark on a risky venture. They're also adept at handling contests that involve will and strength, whether on the gridiron or in the boardroom. Burn candles or incense to honor these elementals.

Ondines (Undines)

Ondines are water spirits. Mermaids and water nymphs fall into this category. These beautiful but sometimes temperamental beings relate best to sensitive, artistic, and psychic people. Invite them to assist you when you're doing love spells. They can also help you with emotional issues and situations that require keen intuition. Ondines are fond of perfume—pour a few drops in a stream, lake, or other body of water as a thank-you gift.

As representatives of the natural world, elementals frown on people who disrespect or harm the earth or its creatures. To win the elementals' favor, treat animals, plants, and all of our planet's inhabitants kindly.

> "[I]n the solid earth element live spiritual beings of an elemental kind who are very much more clever than human beings. Even a person of extreme astuteness intellectually is no match for these beings . . . One could say that just as man consists of flesh and blood so do these beings consist of cleverness, of super-cleverness . . . We may take pleasure in a red rose or feel enchanted when trees unfold their foliage. But these beings go with the fluid which as sap rises in the rose bush and partici-pate in the redness of the blossoms."
> —RUDOLF STEINER, "THE ELEMENTAL WORLD AND THE FUTURE OF MANKIND," THE GENERAL ANTHROPOSOPHICAL SOCIETY, 1922

Spirits of all sorts populate our earth and the universe beyond. The ancient Greeks believed that spirits known as dryads lived in trees, and that if you cut down a tree the dryad would die. Early Romans believed that beings called nymphs occupied all the waters of the world. You could say that everything in our world embodies spirit—and just to be on the safe side, assume that spirits abide everywhere, even though you may not see them.

Ancestors, ghosts, fairies, mythic creatures, and other supernatural entities have intrigued us since the dawn of time. We've sought to appease them, woo them, avoid their displeasure, and solicit their aid. Spellworkers today still do so. If you choose to do spellwork with spirits, it's a good idea to familiarize yourself with the beings you wish to contact. Some are nice guys, some aren't—and many can be just a bit slippery. The realms in which they function aren't the same as ours, nor do they abide by the same rules we do.

Usually you're better off calling on angels and eschewing demons in any sort of spellwork. Both exist, and both are willing to work with you. But before you invite any spirit to assist you, remember an old saying among magicians: Don't raise any power you can't put down.

Chapter 8

TIMING SPELLS FOR BEST RESULTS

"To every thing there is a season, and a time to every purpose under the heaven."

—Ecclesiastes 3.1, King James Bible

You've heard the saying "timing is everything," right? In spellwork, sometimes *when* you cast a spell can be just as important as *how*. Think of it this way. Casting a spell is like planting seeds. In order for seeds to grow into healthy plants, you must sow them during optimal conditions. The same holds true for spells. Of course, if you feel a pressing need to do a spell or sense that the energies around you are compatible with your intention, by all means go ahead.

ASTROLOGY AND MAGICK

When doing magick spells, it's a good idea to take celestial influences into account in order to choose the most auspicious times to perform spells and rituals. The sun and moon, and their ever-changing relationships to our planet, have fascinated human beings since the beginning of time. Our ancestors noticed that the sun's apparent movement brought about the seasons and that the moon's phases altered the tides and affected fertility in both humans and animals. Even today, we can easily see how solar and lunar forces operate in everyday life.

The ancients believed gods and goddesses inhabited the heavenly bodies. From their celestial abodes, they governed every facet of life on earth. Each deity—and each planet—possessed certain characteristics and powers. Modern astrologers don't usually think of the planets as the homes of god/desses; however, they still connect each of the celestial spheres with specific properties, influences, and powers that affect human and earthly existence.

Planetary Powers

Aligning yourself with planetary powers that support the nature of your spells can improve the effectiveness of your magickal workings. The following table shows each planet's areas of influence. (Note: For convenience, astrologers often lump the sun and moon under the broad heading of "planets" although, of course, we know they're not.)

Planet	Areas of Influence
Sun	Sense of self/identity, public image, career, creativity, leadership, well-being, masculine power
Moon	Emotions, intuition, dreams, home/domestic life, family/children, feminine power
Mercury	Communication, mental skill/activity, learning, travel, commerce
Venus	Love, relationships, social interactions, art, creativity, beauty, women

Mars	Action, vitality/strength, competition, courage, men
Jupiter	Growth/expansion, good luck, knowledge, travel
Saturn	Limitations, responsibility, work/business, stability/permanence
Uranus	Change, independence, sudden or unexpected situations, unconventional ideas or behavior
Neptune	Intuition, dreams, imagination/creativity, the spirit realm
Pluto	Hidden power/forces, transformation, death and rebirth

When you're doing spells, you may want to refer to this table. Venus's energy, for instance, can enhance love spells. Jupiter's expansive power can be an asset when you're doing spells for career success or financial growth. You can use the planets' symbols on candles, in talismans and amulets, and lots of other ways.

PLANETS AND SYMBOLS			
Planet/Node	**Symbol**	**Planet/Node**	**Symbol**
Sun	☉	Jupiter	♃
Moon	☾	Saturn	♄
Mercury	☿	Uranus	♅
Venus	♀	Neptune	♆
Mars	♂	Pluto	♀

You may also wish to consult an astrologer or check an ephemeris (tables of daily planetary movements) to determine when the celestial energies are favorable for your magickal workings.

Power Days

The heavenly bodies also rule the days of the week. By casting a spell on the day that corresponds to your intention—based on the deity who presides over the day—you can increase your potential for success. Most love spells, for instance, should be done on Friday because Venus, the planet of love and relationships, governs that day. Perform spells to bring success or money on Thursday, when Jupiter encourages growth.

Day of the Week	Ruling Planet/Deity
Monday	Moon
Tuesday	Mars
Wednesday	Mercury
Thursday	Jupiter
Friday	Venus
Saturday	Saturn
Sunday	Sun

Your Personal Best

When's the best time for you to cast a spell? On your birthday. On that special day each year, the sun shines brightly on you (even if it's raining outdoors) and spotlights your unique talents and abilities. Its energy illuminates and enhances whatever you undertake. As a result, whatever spells you do on your birthday have a better than usual chance of succeeding.

Planets and Signs

Each planet rules one or more signs of the zodiac. You probably know your birth sign—that's the astrological sign in which the sun was positioned on the day you were born. What you may not know, though, is that the moon and all the planets in our solar system also spend periods of time in each of the twelve signs of the zodiac and they continually move through these signs/sectors of the heavens. These signs "color" the energy of the planets. Therefore, it's good to check the positions of the planets when you're doing spells—especially the placements of the sun and moon. In Part II, I frequently advise doing spells when the sun or moon is in a particular astrological sign, in order to tip the scales in your favor. The following table shows the connections between the planets and the signs they govern.

Planet	Zodiac Sign(s)
Sun	Leo
Moon	Cancer
Mercury	Gemini, Virgo
Venus	Taurus, Libra
Mars	Aries
Jupiter	Sagittarius
Saturn	Capricorn
Uranus	Aquarius
Neptune	Pisces
Pluto	Scorpio

Now, refer back to the table presented earlier in this chapter that lists the planets and their areas of influence. When the sun or moon is positioned in a sign, it takes on some of the characteristics of that sign and the planet that rules the sign, which can be important in spellwork. For example, it's usually best to do love spells when the sun or moon is in Taurus or Libra—signs ruled by the planet Venus. If you're doing a travel spell, consider casting it when the sun or moon is in Gemini or Sagittarius.

The moon remains in a sign for about two and a half days and completes a circuit of all twelve zodiac signs each month. Check an ephemeris or an online astrology site to determine which days will support your objectives.

MOON MAGICK

In early agrarian cultures, our ancestors planted crops and bred animals in accordance with the moon's cycles. Today, we can still see the moon's influence on fertility cycles, crop growth, the ocean's tides, and mundane affairs. In terms of casting spells, the moon is the most important of the heavenly bodies to consider. Magick practitioners often time their spells to correspond to the movements of this so-called "lesser light," perhaps because the moon rules intuition and the emotions, two parts of the psyche that strongly influence magick.

Farmers' Almanac

For almost 200 years, the *Farmers' Almanac* has published information about lunar cycles. It's not uncommon for farmers who employ advanced technical methods to also take the *Almanac*'s advice when planting and harvesting crops. Spellworkers, too, realize that you can reap greater benefits if you sow seeds (physically or symbolically) when the moon's position supports growth.

The New Moon

The new moon supports beginnings: the inception of new ideas, plans, projects, relationships, and activities. Now is the time to plant symbolic seeds that represent whatever you wish to create in your life. Cast spells to launch a new business, begin a relationship, or start a family. As the moon moves toward its full phase, you can watch your endeavor develop. The new moon is a good time to do divination, too.

The Waxing Phase

The moon's waxing phase—the two weeks between the new and full moons—represents a period of growth. This is the best time to do spells designed to expand a business, attract new people, and encourage prosperity. If, for instance, you wish to earn more money or get a promotion at work, do a spell during the waxing moon. As the moon's light grows, so will your fortune.

The Full Moon

The full moon represents the time of culmination and harvest. Under the moon's bright light, you can see (or at least start to see) the results of whatever you initiated two weeks ago, during the new moon, and begin reaping the benefits. You have more clarity now to understand how your goals are shaping up and what steps you need to take (if any) to bring them to fruition. Things that were hidden before may now come to light.

The Waning Phase

During the two weeks from the full moon to the next new moon, the moon "wanes" and appears to diminish in size from our vantage point here on Earth. This is a good time to do spells that involve decrease or letting go. This two-week period is perfect for spells to break old romantic ties, lose weight, eliminate bad habits, and reduce responsibilities at home or work. As the moon visibly shrinks, so will the conditions you've targeted with your magick.

Black and Blue Moons

When a month contains two full moons, the second is called a "blue moon." When two new moons occur in one month, the second is known as a "black moon." In these instances, the second one is considered more powerful than a regular new or full moon, so spells you do now may manifest more quickly.

Keeping a Lunar Journal

You may find it useful to keep track of the moon's phases for a few months, to get a sense of how the energy shifts and how it affects you. In a notebook or computer file, write a paragraph or so about how you feel during each lunar phase—describe your emotions, experiences, thoughts, and anything unusual or especially meaningful that happens. You might also wish to record your dreams and examine them in connection with the moon's position.

If you're recording your magickal work in a grimoire or book of shadows, be sure to note the moon's phase and its zodiac sign at the time you cast each spell. This practice will enable you to keep track of the moon's impact on your spells, so you can work more successfully with lunar power in the future.

ESBATS

Witches often come together for esbats, or meetings of covens, usually on full and/or new moons, to enjoy community and fellowship. Each full moon has its own unique characteristics, often based on seasonal energies. Esbat rituals draw upon nature's patterns, as well as mythology, cultural traditions, and astrology. Whether or not your magickal practice involves other people, you may wish to mark the full moons with rituals and/or spellwork. The following list briefly describes some of the attributes of each full moon. (Note that different cultures call the moons by different names.)

1. January—Known as the Cold, Frost, Ice, and Quiet Moon, it marks a time for renewal, discovery, resolve, and focusing on your purpose. Now is the time to set goals and to do spells for wealth and prosperity.
2. February—Called the Wild, Snow, Ice, and Starving Moon, it represents a period of healing and purification. Spells that prepare you for initiation, encourage healing or new growth, or foster physical or financial well-being are appropriate at this time.
3. March—The Storm, Wind, or Death Moon ushers in a time of change and awakening after a bleak, dormant period. Goals set under January's Cold Moon now begin to manifest. Do spells for personal growth and change now.
4. April—The Seed, Water, Growing, or Awakening Moon is a time of opening to new opportunities and experiences. Do spells for love, cleansing, growth, and strength at this time.

The Modern Witchcraft Spell Book

5. May—Known as the Hare, Bright, Grass, and Corn-planting Moon, it encourages joy, pleasure, sexuality, and fertility. This is a good time to do love spells, as well as spells for healing from emotional trauma and loss.

6. June—During the Honey, Mead, Planting, or Horse Moon, focus on strengthening relationships of all kinds: love, family, friendship, etc. This is also a good time to do spells to enhance communication and domestic harmony.

7. July—The Wort, Raspberry, or Rose Moon represents a time of maturation and fulfillment. Spells for protection and prosperity can benefit from the energy of this full moon.

8. August—This harvest moon, known as the Barley, Gathering, or Lightning Moon, is a time for gathering together all that holds meaning for you. Celebrate your blessings now and show gratitude, which will bring more blessings your way. Work with others of like mind during this time to share ideas, goals, and information.

9. September—The Harvest, Singing, or Spiderweb Moon is another period of reaping rewards for your efforts, and for seeing your dreams come to fruition. Give thanks for goals realized, projects completed, and wisdom gained. Focus on completion and bringing your life into balance.

10. October—During the Blood, Harvest, or Leaf-falling Moon, release old patterns and clear away emotional/psychic debris. Do spells to help you let go of whatever or whoever is standing in your way of fulfillment. This is also a time to remember and honor loved ones who have moved on to another realm of existence.

11. November—The Snow, Dark, or Tree Moon is a time to look beyond the mundane world, into the magickal one. Scry to gaze into the future; do divination to gain guidance and wisdom that will aid you in the coming months. Open your mind to receive prophecies of things to come.

12. December—Under the Dark, Cold, or Long Night Moon, release your fears and banish those things in your life that are harmful or no longer useful. This is a time for silence, meditation, and introspection. Do spells to break old bonds, overcome obstacles, and end self-limiting habits/behaviors.

Whether you belong to a group of magick workers or are a solitary practitioner, you will experience during full moon nights the sense of community and fellowship of like-minded people. You can be certain that on any full moon, people around the world are casting circles and performing spells, celebrating and chanting, scrying and meditating. You are an integral part of this global community. By realizing your part in the whole, you will bring yourself into closer connection with your fellow beings and the Divine.

SABBATS

Our ancestors divided the sun's annual cycle, known as the Wheel of the Year, into eight periods of approximately six weeks each. Each "spoke" in the Wheel corresponds to a particular degree in the zodiac. Witches and other pagans refer to these dates as *sabbats*, and celebrate them as holidays (or holy days). These high-energy days offer special opportunities for performing magick spells and rituals.

Samhain

Better known as Halloween or All Hallow's Eve, this holy day is usually observed on the night of October 31. For witches, Samhain is a time to remember and honor loved ones who have passed over to the other side (hence the connection with death). You may also wish to contact spirits in other realms of existence on this eve, or request guidance from ancestors or guardians. Because the "veil" that separates the seen and unseen worlds is thinnest at Samhain, many people like to do tarot or rune readings now to gain insight into the future. Perform spells to break old bonds and shed old habits on Samhain. For example, on a piece of paper write down something you want to release from your life, then burn the paper in your cauldron or a ritual fire.

Yule, the Winter Solstice

Yule is celebrated on the day of the winter solstice, which usually occurs between December 20 and December 22. This is the shortest day of the year in the Northern Hemisphere, the time when the earth is farthest away from the sun in her orbit through space. Because Yule marks the turning point at which the days begin to lengthen again, witches hail it as the "return of the light." To celebrate, light candles to represent the sun and burn a Yule log (usually oak, which symbolizes strength and longevity). Save a piece of the log to start your Yule fire next year. Do spells for rebirth and new beginnings on this sabbat.

Imbolc, Brigid's Day, or Candlemas

This sabbat honors Brigid, the beloved Celtic goddess of healing, smithcraft, and poetry. Her holiday begins on the evening of January 31 and concludes on February 2. At this time, daylight is increasing and the promise of spring is in the air. Thus, Imbolc is considered a time of hope and renewal. Brigid is one of the fertility goddesses, often depicted stirring a cauldron, and *imbolc* means "in the belly." Witches connect her with all forms of creativity, so this sabbat is a good time to engage your own creative urges. Do spells to launch new ventures, kindle inspiration for a project, or spark your imagination.

Ostara, the Spring Equinox

Usually celebrated around March 21, Ostara marks the first day of spring, ushering in warmer weather and longer days in the Northern Hemisphere. The earth awakens from her long winter's sleep and new life begins to emerge once more. This sabbat celebrates the triumph of life over death, as well as fertility and creativity. A time for planting seeds—literally or figuratively—Ostara's energy supports spells for beginnings. Consider planting herbs and flowers now to use in future spells. You may also want to craft talismans to attract good fortune.

Beltane

Witches usually celebrate Beltane on May 1, when flowers bloom profusely and crops begin sprouting in the fields. The sabbat marks a period of fruitfulness, and honors sexuality and fertility. An old tradition says that on Beltane women who wished to become pregnant should build a small fire in a cauldron, and then jump over it. Do love spells on this sabbat—fashion good luck charms to attract a new partner or improve an existing relationship. This is also a good time to tap the earth's fertility for prosperity magick—plant herbs such as mint and parsley to use in money spells.

Midsummer, the Summer Solstice

In the Northern Hemisphere, the summer solstice is the longest day of the year, usually around June 21. This is a time of abundance, when the earth puts forth her bounty in all its radiance. Tap this period of fullness to boost the power of spells for wealth, success, or recognition. Legend says you can communicate with the elementals and fairies now, and solicit their help in spellwork (see Chapter 7). Midsummer is also a good time to collect herbs, flowers, and other plants to use in magick spells throughout the year.

Lughnasadh or Lammas

Named for the Irish Celtic god Lugh (Lew in Wales), Lughnasadh (pronounced *LOO-nah-sah*) is usually celebrated on August 1. It is the first of the harvest festivals; our ancestors saw it as a time to reap the fruits of their labors and to begin preparing for the winter months ahead. As you enjoy the earth's bounty, remember to show gratitude for your blessings. This is a good time to do spells for health and protection, and to concoct herbal potions from fresh, healthy plants.

Mabon, the Autumn Equinox

Usually occurring around September 22, the autumn equinox is a time of balance and harmony, when day and night are of equal length. During this second harvest festival, witches take stock of the year's successes and failures, and give thanks for the good things in their lives. Honor your accomplishments now and reassess situations that didn't turn out as you'd hoped. As the year wanes, do spells for letting go, reduction, and endings. Legal spells can also benefit from Maban's energy. This is also a good time to resolve conflict and establish boundaries, in both personal and professional areas.

My book *The Modern Guide to Witchcraft* discusses the Wheel of the Year in greater depth, and includes some of the traditions surrounding these sabbats. It also offers suggestions for celebrating these special days.

When *Not* to Cast a Spell

Unless you have a clear goal in mind, don't bother doing a spell. Not only is it a waste of time and energy, it can actually create more problems because the energy generated by your spell lacks focus and bounces around through your life randomly like a pinball. If you're distracted or worried, your state of mind will interfere with your focus and the effects of your spell. Usually it's not a good idea to do a spell when you're ill, either, because your personal energies are unbalanced and that could weaken your spell. You might even send unhealthy vibes into the universe or drain your own vitality. Of course, you may want to do a spell to regain your health; try something gentle, such as a healing bath (see Chapter 13).

As we now move into Part II of this book, you'll notice that I recommend the best time to perform each spell, taking into account the moon's phase and other astrological influences. Usually I suggest more than one option. If a situation warrants immediate action and you can't do a spell on the optimal date, don't despair. Go ahead, and remember that your intention is the most important part of any spell.

PART II

Spells for
ALL REASONS
AND SEASONS

Chapter 9

SPELLS FOR LOVE AND FRIENDSHIP

As you may suspect, love spells are the ones magicians cast most frequently. We even use magickal terms to describe being in love—we feel enchanted, under a spell, bewitched, charmed, and so on. Often when we think of love spells, our minds conjure images of magickal incantations and mysterious potions meant to kindle passion in a person the spell-crafter desires, especially if that person doesn't return the feeling. Fairy tales, poetry, popular songs, and Hollywood perpetuate this idea.

Keep in mind, however, that love spells aren't meant to enchant or bewitch someone into falling in love with you—especially if that certain someone is already involved in a romantic relationship with another person. Although it may be tempting, and more than a few magicians have used magick to manipulate another person, doing so can backfire, sometimes with disastrous results. We all have free will and nothing can violate that will—not even magick or spells. The true purpose of a love spell is to increase your own power and attractiveness, so you draw the individual who's best for you.

If your spell involves someone else, ask his or her permission before casting it. This may not be possible if you're trying to make peace with another person from whom you're separated or if you need to break an unwanted bond between you and someone else. Even then, explain your intentions to that person's higher self and make it clear that you seek only the best for everyone concerned. If it's appropriate, you might invite the other person to participate in your spell. This can be beneficial if your spell is intended to enhance some aspect of an existing relationship, such as heightening the passion or joy between you.

Spells for love are numerous and varied, and before you do any, it's important to define what you want. Are you trying to attract someone? Looking for your soul mate? Hoping to improve your current relationship? The clearer you are in your own mind, and the more specific you can be, the greater your chances of success. The tables in this chapter show which ingredients can lend more power to your love spells.

Steps for Successful Spellcasting

Whenever you cast a spell, remember to use a few tried-and-true measures, as described in Chapter 1. These precautions can help you avoid complications, mix-ups, delays, or disappointments:

1. Remove all distractions.
2. Collect the ingredients and tools you'll use in your spell and cleanse them.
3. Purify and sanctify your space.
4. Quiet your mind.
5. Cast a circle around the area where you'll do your spellworking.
6. Perform the spell.
7. If you've called upon deities or spirits to assist you, thank and release them.
8. Open the circle.
9. Store your tools in a safe place until you need them again.

COLORS FOR LOVE SPELLS

Try to incorporate the colors red (for passion), pink (for affection), and/or purple (for romance) into your love spells. The most popular ways to do this are to burn candles or craft talisman pouches in these colors. You may also want to wear red and/or pink gemstones as talismans, or add red, pink, or purple flower petals to mojo bags, ritual baths, sachets, or potions. Many of the spells in this chapter draw upon these color associations.

INGREDIENTS FOR LOVE SPELLS

Gemstones

Carnelian: Stimulates sexual desire

Diamond: Deepens commitment and trust in a love relationship

Garnet: Increases love and passion

Opal: Aids love and seduction

Pearl: Encourages love, happiness, and emotional balance

Quartz (rose): Attracts romance, affection, and friendship

Flowers

Daisy: Inspires playfulness in love and friendship

Geranium (rose-colored): Boosts fertility and love

Jasmine: Encourages love, harmony, seduction, and sensuality

Myrtle: Brings luck in love

Rose: Attracts love and friendship; pink for affection, red for passion

Essential Oils/Incense

Jasmine: Encourages love, harmony, seduction, and sensuality

Musk: Heightens sensuality and sexuality

Patchouli: Boosts passion and sensuality

Rose: Attracts love and friendship

Ylang ylang: Increases sensuality and attractiveness

Herbs and Spices

Cayenne: Sparks sexuality and desire

Ginger: Stimulates romance, excitement, and sexuality

Marjoram: Blesses a new union and brings happiness

Vanilla: Encourages a more joyful and lighthearted approach to love

A SIMPLE SPELL TO ATTRACT LOVE

This quick-and-easy love spell requires only a handful of rose petals (preferably given to you by a friend or loved one, so they're already imbued with good energy). Take them outside your house or apartment and scatter them on the walkway leading to your home, while you say aloud:

> *"Love find your way.*
> *Love come to stay!"*

Continue repeating the incantation until you reach your door. Save one rose petal to carry with you as a talisman to encourage love to follow you into your home.

SPELL TO ATTRACT YOUR SOUL MATE

You're looking for that special person, the one and only, your ideal mate who is right for you in every way. But where do you begin? By casting a spell, of course. This one sends out the message that you are open to receiving love—and your perfect partner will pick up your vibes.

INGREDIENTS/TOOLS:
- 1 red rose
- 1 vase of cold water
- 1 ballpoint pen
- 1 pink votive candle
- 1 red votive candle
- A few drops of ylang-ylang essential oil
- 1 copper bowl
- Matches or a lighter

BEST TIME TO PERFORM THE SPELL:
- On the new moon, preferably on a Friday, or when the sun or moon is in Libra

Place the rose, which symbolizes the love you're looking for, in a vase of water and set it on your altar. Use the ballpoint pen to inscribe the letter X—the Norse rune for love—on the candles. Anoint the candles, which represent you and your soul mate, with the essential oil. (Pink is the color of love and affection, red the color of passion.) Put the candles together in the bowl and place it on your altar. Light the candles and say aloud:

> *"Winds of love, come to me,*
> *Bring my soul mate, I decree.*
> *As I wish, so mote it be."*

Imagine yourself with your soul mate. Make your visualization as detailed and vivid as possible. Feel this person's presence forming in the air around you. Let the candles burn all the way down, so the pink and red wax flow together in the bowl. While the wax is still warm, shape it with your fingers to form a heart, mingling the pink and red. Empty the vase of cold water into the bowl so the wax doesn't stick, and then remove the wax heart. If you know feng shui, put the wax heart in your relationship sector; otherwise place it in your bedroom. Allow the rose petals to dry. Save them for other spells.

SPELL TO ATTRACT FRIENDS

You've got to have friends in this world. For many people, friends are just as important as a primary partner. Friends bring out your best side, share your interests, pitch in when times are tough, and create a community in which you can thrive.

INGREDIENTS/TOOLS:
- Several ribbons

BEST TIME TO PERFORM THE SPELL:
- During the waxing moon, preferably when the sun or moon is in Gemini or Aquarius

This is a good spell to perform when you move into a new neighborhood or enter a new school and don't know anybody. Collect several ribbons in various colors that you like. Each ribbon represents a friend. Tie the ribbons to the branches of a tree. As you tie each ribbon, focus on attracting a new friend into your life and say aloud: "I now have a friend whom I love, respect, trust, and enjoy." Repeat until you've tied all the ribbons on the tree, then thank the tree for adding its positive energy to your spell.

SPELL TO ENHANCE A ROMANTIC RELATIONSHIP

Is something lacking in your relationship? Do you seek more romance, harmony, joy, passion? Choose the ingredients that will increase what you desire. Pink candles, for example, represent love and affection, whereas red ones represent passion. Select the aromatic oil you like best—see the table at the beginning of this chapter for suggestions.

INGREDIENTS/TOOLS:
- 2 pink or red candles in candleholders
- A few drops of rose, ylang-ylang, jasmine, gardenia, vanilla, or patchouli essential oil
- Deck of tarot cards
- Matches or a lighter

BEST TIME TO PERFORM THE SPELL:
- During the waxing moon, preferably on a Friday, or when the sun or moon is in Taurus or Libra

During the waxing moon, anoint the candles with the essential oil. Put a dot of oil on your heart to open it. From your deck of tarot cards, select the king and the queen of cups (which stand for you and your partner) and the nine of cups (the wish card). Place the candles on your altar, and lay the three cards face up between the candles.

Light the candles and state your wish. Be specific. Imagine it coming true. After a few minutes, extinguish the candles and place them in the area where you and your beloved will be spending time together.

Whenever you're together in that room, make sure these candles are burning.

Variations on Tarot Spells

You can also choose tarot cards according to your astrological sun sign to represent you and the person you love. Wands correlate with fire signs (Aries, Leo, Sagittarius). Pentacles are associated with earth signs (Taurus, Virgo, Capricorn). Swords relate to air signs (Gemini, Libra, Aquarius). Cups are linked with water signs (Cancer, Scorpio, Pisces). If you're at least twenty-one years old, select a king or queen from the suit that corresponds to your sign to symbolize you and the other person. If you're under twenty-one or doing a spell for younger people, use the pages of the appropriate suits.

RELATIONSHIP RESCUE PIE

Even a really great relationship hits some slumps once in a while. Whenever your relationship is in need of a pick-me-up, whip up an apple pie to bring more sweetness into your union. Apples represent health and love. Cinnamon is a sweet-and-spicy love herb, vanilla inspires love and peace, and ginger stimulates whatever it touches. Make sure to hold loving thoughts in your mind while you bake this delicious treat.

SERVES 6

INGREDIENTS/TOOLS:

- 6 medium tart apples, peeled and sliced thin
- ½ teaspoon ginger
- ½ teaspoon cinnamon
- ½ teaspoon nutmeg (or to taste)
- ½ teaspoon vanilla
- ¼ cup flour
- 2 prepared piecrusts for a 9" pie, or make crusts from scratch
- 2 tablespoons butter

- On a Friday night, during the waxing moon, or when the moon is in Libra or Taurus

1. Preheat the oven to 425°F.
2. Toss the apple slices with the spices, vanilla, and flour, then put them into the bottom of the piecrust. Dot the top of the apples evenly with bits of butter.
3. Put the other half of the piecrust over the top of the pie, securing it at the edges while saying:

"Secured within,
My magick begins.
Sweeten our love,
With blessings from above."

4. Gently draw a heart in the top of the pie using a fork so that energy bakes into the crust.
5. Bake the pie in the preheated oven for about 45 minutes, or until the crust is brown and apple juice is bubbling through the heart pattern. Enjoy eating the pie with your beloved.

THE DRINK OF LOVE

Japanese scientist Masaru Emoto discovered that water picks up the vibrations of pictures, words, thoughts, and emotions that come into contact with it. The water holds on to those impressions—and when you drink the imprinted water, your body absorbs the energies. This spell uses the lovely imagery from The Lovers card in your favorite tarot deck to fill you with loving feelings.

- The Lovers card from a tarot deck
- 1 glass of spring water
- 1 silver (or silver plate) spoon
- 1 drop of melted honey or a pinch of sugar

BEST TIME TO PERFORM THE SPELL:

- On a Friday night, during the waxing moon, or when the sun or moon is in Libra

Place the tarot card face up on a windowsill where the moon will shine on it. Set the glass of water on top of the card and leave it overnight. The image of the card will be imprinted into the water. In the morning, use a silver spoon to stir the honey or sugar into the glass to sweeten the water and, symbolically, your relationship. Drink the water with your partner to strengthen the love between you.

LOVE BATH

A luxurious bath can soothe mind, body, and spirit, and help you let go of the stress of the day. This spell cleanses you of tension or unpleasantness in a love relationship, so you can enjoy the positive things and open yourself to more happiness.

INGREDIENTS/TOOLS:

- A tub filled with comfortably hot water
- 1 cup of bath salts
- A few drops of jasmine, ylang-ylang, patchouli, or rose essential oil
- The rest of the rose petals left from the Spell to Attract Your Soul Mate
- 1 red or pink candle in a candleholder
- Matches or a lighter
- Romantic music

BEST TIME TO PERFORM THE SPELL:

- On a Friday night, during the waxing moon

As you fill your bathtub with water, sprinkle the bath salts into it. Bath salts act as a purifying agent, dispersing any unwanted vibrations. It's also a symbol of the earth element, which is associated with stability, security, and sensuality. Add the essential oil to the bath water, then scatter the rose petals on top. Light the candle and turn on the music.

Get into the tub and soak pleasantly, as you think loving thoughts about your partner. If you don't yet have a romantic partner, think positive thoughts about the person you intend to attract. If you have a lover, invite him or her to join you in the love bath.

SPELL TO MEND A ROMANTIC RIFT

A lovers' quarrel has left you and your partner at odds. Maybe you've said or done things you wish you could take back. Pride, hurt feelings, anger, and other destructive emotions may be preventing you from making up. How can you mend the rift between you? By casting a magick spell, of course. The key to this spell's success is focusing your mind on positive images only.

INGREDIENTS/TOOLS:
- 1 clear quartz crystal
- 1 ballpoint pen
- 1 piece of paper
- A few drops of jasmine essential oil
- 2 pink candles
- Candleholders
- Matches or a lighter

BEST TIME TO PERFORM THE SPELL:
- As soon as possible

Wash the quartz crystal with mild soap and water, then pat it dry. On the piece of paper write down everything you like, admire, and enjoy about your partner. Include his or her positive qualities, things about the relationship that you're grateful for, good times you've shared, and so on.

When you've finished, put a drop of oil on each corner of the paper and fold it three times.

Use the ballpoint pen to inscribe your name on one of the candles and your beloved's name on the other. Dress the candles by rubbing a little oil on them (not on the wicks). Put the candles in their holders and position them on your altar, a table, or other flat surface, so they are about a foot apart. Lay the folded piece of paper between the candles and set the crystal on top of the paper. Light the candles.

Close your eyes and bring to mind an image of your partner. Say to that image: "I honor the divine within you. I forgive you and I forgive myself. I am grateful for all the good times we've known together. I bless you and love you." Let go of all anger, resentment, recrimination, criticism, and so forth that you have held toward your partner. Don't mentally rehash the problems that led to the rift; entertain only positive thoughts and feelings. When you're ready, open your eyes and snuff out the candles. If necessary, repeat the spell the next day, only this time move the two candles a little closer together. Do this spell daily, moving the candles closer each time, until you've mended the rift between you.

A SPELL FOR FIDELITY

This spell encourages fidelity, but before casting it consider your reasons for doing so. Do you just want to strengthen the bond of trust between you and a partner? Or do you suspect that your significant other is being unfaithful? If so, do you really want to remain with this person?

INGREDIENTS/TOOLS:
- 4 votive candles (1 yellow, 1 red, 1 blue, and 1 green) in glass containers
- 1 object that represents your lover
- 1 object that represents you
- Matches or a lighter

BEST TIME TO PERFORM THE SPELL:
- On the full moon

Be sure to position your candles in a safe spot, where they can't ignite anything flammable. Place the yellow candle in the east within the space where you'll do your spell. Set the red one in the south, the blue one in the west, and the green one in the north. This defines the perimeter of your circle, and as you light each candle—moving clockwise from the east—you cast the circle. But before you do this, make sure that you and the objects you've chosen to represent you and your partner are within the circle.

Face east and light the yellow candle. Breathe deeply and imagine your intellect as lucid, crystalline, capable of making good decisions. Face south and light the red candle. Envision yourself and your lover passionately embracing. Face west and light the blue candle, as you sense loving feelings flowing between you and your partner. Face north, light the green candle, and imagine a strong bond of devotion, respect, and caring uniting you. When you have finished lighting the candles, stand facing the east and say:

"Winds of the east and the mind, keep [name of person]'s thoughts with me. So mote it be."

Turn to face south and say:

"Fires of the south and passion, keep [name] close to me. So mote it be."

Face west and say:

"Waters of our hearts, never do us part. So mote it be."

Face north and say:

"Forces of the earth, keep our bodies together now and evermore. So mote it be."

Move to the center of the circle and say:

"This spell is done in harmony with Divine Will, our own true wills, and with good to all."

To open the circle, snuff out the candles in the reverse order, moving counterclockwise, then bury the remains together in your backyard. If you live in an apartment, put the candles in a wooden box and place it under your bed.

MAGICK NECKLACE TO STIMULATE PASSION

Do you seem to be losing interest in your partner? Perhaps you long for the day when your love affair was passionate and fun. Still, you're not ready to give up on the relationship. This talisman draws upon the energies of gemstones to help rekindle your enthusiasm. It's also a pretty piece of jewelry.

INGREDIENTS/TOOLS:
- Carnelian or garnet beads (as many as you want to use)
- Opal beads (as many as you want to use)
- Pink pearls (as many as you want to use)
- Jeweler's wire, enough to make a necklace
- A few drops of ylang-ylang or jasmine essential oil

BEST TIME TO PERFORM THE SPELL:
- During the waxing moon, preferably on a Tuesday or Friday, or when the sun or moon is in Aries, Taurus, or Scorpio

Wash all the gemstones with mild soap and water, then pat them dry. Begin stringing the beads on the jeweler's wire. String the stones in any combination, as many of each as you feel you need. Carnelians and garnets spark passion. Opals encourage romance. Pearls promote emotional balance, harmony, and joy.

As you work, remember the good times you've enjoyed with your beloved. Concentrate especially on the passionate, romantic, and exciting moments between you. Think about all the things you admire and like about your partner. Don't let your mind stray to negative thoughts. Make the necklace as long as you like. When you've strung all the beads, dot each bead with a little essential oil. Allow the scent to imprint itself on your subconscious. Wear your magick necklace to reawaken passion in your partnership. Whenever you feel your enthusiasm waning, finger the beads to remind you of your intention.

COMMITMENT TALISMAN

Is the one you love commitment phobic? Are you having trouble moving your relationship to the next level? This talisman helps deepen and stabilize the feelings between you. However, in order to make this spell succeed you'll have to act in a way that seems contrary to your intentions: Stop pushing for a commitment and give your beloved the space he or she needs.

INGREDIENTS/TOOLS:
- 1 small piece of rose quartz
- 1 small piece of smoky quartz
- 1 small piece of carnelian
- 1 small piece of hematite
- 1 gold, silver, or copper ring
- Rose or jasmine incense
- Incense burner
- Matches or a lighter
- 1 pink or rose silk pouch
- 1 of your hairs
- 1 of your beloved's hairs
- Rose, jasmine, and gardenia petals
- 1 red ribbon
- Saltwater

BEST TIME TO PERFORM THE SPELL:
- On a Friday during the waxing moon, preferably when the sun or moon is in Taurus or Libra

Wash the stones and the ring with mild soap and water, then pat them dry. Fit the incense into its burner and light it. Put the 4 stones into the silk pouch. Tie the hairs around the ring if they're long enough; if not, simply put the hairs and the ring into the pouch. Add the flower petals.

Close the pouch with the red ribbon, tying 8 knots. As you tie each knot, repeat this incantation:

"I love you and you love me
Together we shall always be
And live in perfect harmony."

When you've finished, sprinkle the talisman with saltwater then hold it in the incense smoke for a few moments to charge your charm. Say aloud: "This is done in harmony with Divine Will, our own true wills, and for the good of all."

If you know feng shui, place the talisman in the relationship sector of your home; otherwise put it in your bedroom. Now that you've completed the spell, let go and let the universe take over.

SPELL FOR A PEACEFUL RELATIONSHIP

No matter how hard you try to get along, you and your partner always seem to end up fighting about something. It's uncanny how you manage to push each other's buttons. This spell helps to sweeten the energy between you to promote peace and harmony in your relationship.

INGREDIENTS/TOOLS:
- 1 shell
- 1 oblong stone
- 1 cauldron, large ashtray, incense burner, or other fireproof container
- 1 cone of gardenia incense
- Dried pink rose petals
- A dab of honey
- Matches or a lighter
- 1 pink cloth pouch, preferably silk or velvet

The Modern Witchcraft Spell Book

- On a Friday, preferably when the sun or moon is in Libra

Wash the shell and stone with mild soap and water, then pat them dry. Set the fireproof container on your altar or in another safe place. Put the incense in the center of the container, then sprinkle the rose petals around the incense. Rub a little honey on the shell and the stone, then lay both in the container—the shell represents the feminine force, the oblong stone symbolizes the male force.

Call to mind your lover's face. Light the incense. As it burns, chant this incantation aloud three times as if you were speaking to your partner:

"Between me and thee
May there always be
Love, peace, and harmony."

Allow the incense to burn down completely. When everything has cooled, put the shell, stone, rose petals, and ashes into the pink pouch. Place the pouch under your pillow or between the mattress and box spring of your bed to encourage positive feelings.

SPELL TO INCREASE YOUR ATTRACTIVENESS

You can use this spell to attract a romantic partner, or to get the attention of people you'd like to have as friends. It enhances your physical beauty, your communication skills, or other qualities that others find attractive.

INGREDIENTS/TOOLS:
- 1 ripe strawberry
- 1 small bowl or saucer
- 1 fork

BEST TIME TO PERFORM THE SPELL:
- During the waxing moon, preferably on a Thursday or Friday, or when the moon is in Libra

Hold the strawberry as you visualize people looking twice at you, complimenting you on your appearance, approaching you to chat, and so on. Put the strawberry in the bowl or saucer and mash it gently with the fork. Then anoint your lips with the strawberry juice. Eat the crushed strawberry sensually, enjoying the feeling of the pulp on your tongue, the seeds between your teeth, and the sweetness of the juice.

Say aloud:

"The words I speak,
The smiles I smile,
Be made sweet.
As bee to flower,
As honey to fly,
I draw you nigh."

SPELL TO SPARK ROMANCE

This spell increases your "sparkle" in an intimate situation. It can help you draw a new love to you or add zest to an existing relationship.

INGREDIENTS/TOOLS:
- Champagne (or sparkling apple cider)
- 1 chalice (or pretty wineglass)
- 3 drops rosewater

BEST TIME TO PERFORM THE SPELL:
- During the waxing moon, preferably on a Friday or when the moon is in Libra

Pour the champagne into your chalice or glass. Add the first drop of rosewater to the glass and say aloud: "I dazzle."

Add the second drop of rosewater to your chalice or glass as you say: "I sparkle."

Add the third and final drop of rosewater and say: "Romance me!"

Swirl the champagne in the glass gently to blend the rosewater. Drink the champagne, visualizing exactly how you wish to be attractive and what sort of experience you'd like to enjoy with a partner. See yourself and your partner as happy and fulfilled. Make the visualization as vivid as possible.

VARIATIONS TO TRY:
- Float a fresh red rose petal on the surface of the champagne.
- Double the ingredients to serve two people, and drink it with your partner.
- Serve chocolate-covered strawberries to further enhance the atmosphere for love.

A SPELL TO SAFEGUARD LOVE

This spell uses three spellcasting techniques—verbal, written, and physical—to renew, strengthen, preserve, and energize your love.

INGREDIENTS/TOOLS:
- Red or purple construction paper (red and purple are colors of passion and romance respectively)
- Rose oil
- Scissors
- Glue or tape
- 1 picture of you and your mate
- 1 pen that writes red ink

BEST TIME TO PERFORM THE SPELL:
- Anytime

Dab the paper with the rose oil, while saying:

"Rose of love, this spell is begun
I and [name of your partner] will always be one!"

Cut the paper in the shape of a heart. In the middle of the paper heart affix the picture(s) of yourself and your beloved. Write your names underneath. Put the heart in the relationship sector of your home (if you know feng shui) or in your bedroom to keep love alive.

Chapter 10

MONEY AND ABUNDANCE SPELLS

Who couldn't use a little more money—or maybe a whole lot more? We all know that money can't buy love, health, friendship, happiness, or respect—but prosperity sure beats poverty. In our material world money may not be everything, but it's essential to our day-to-day existence. Of course, abundance consists of much more than money. You may possess abundant vitality or intellect or creativity—riches that don't depend on and can't be bought with money. However, financial prosperity can provide the space, security, and opportunity for you to express your other gifts, without having to spend the bulk of your time and energy just earning a living.

Are you tired of worrying about bills? Would you like a better living and/or working environment? Do you need more time to devote to your creative pursuits, but don't feel you can afford it? Do you want more financial freedom to travel, further your education, break out of an unhappy domestic situation, or start your own business? The spells in this chapter are designed to help you overcome obstacles to prosperity and to attract abundance of all kinds into your life. The tables that follow show which ingredients can lend more power to your spells—feel free to customize if you choose to make a spell more personal.

Steps for Successful Spellcasting

Whenever you cast a spell, remember to use a few tried-and-true measures, as described in Chapter 1. These precautions can help you avoid complications, mix-ups, delays, or disappointments:

1. Remove all distractions.
2. Collect the ingredients and tools you'll use in your spell and cleanse them.
3. Purify and sanctify your space.
4. Quiet your mind.
5. Cast a circle around the area where you'll do your spellworking.
6. Perform the spell.
7. If you've called upon deities or spirits to assist you, thank and release them.
8. Open the circle.
9. Store your tools in a safe place until you need them again.

COLORS TO USE IN MONEY SPELLS

To enhance the spells you do for money and prosperity, incorporate the colors gold and silver (to symbolize precious metals and coins) and green (the color of paper money in some cultures and the indicator of healthy plant growth). The most popular ways to bring in these colors are to burn candles or craft talisman pouches in these colors. You may also want to wear golden, silvery, or green gemstones as talismans or add golden flower petals to mojo bags, ritual baths, sachets, or potions. Many of the spells in this chapter draw upon these color associations.

INGREDIENTS FOR PROSPERITY SPELLS
Gemstones
Agate (green): Helps stabilize your finances
Aventurine: Attracts wealth and abundance
Quartz abundance crystal: Aids financial growth and attracts abundance of all kinds
Tiger's eye: Increases good fortune and prosperity
Flowers
Daffodil: Attracts good luck
Marigold: Encourages financial gain
Sunflower: Its numerous seeds represent abundance and its sunny yellow petals suggest gold
Tulip: The cuplike shape represents a vessel to hold money and treasures
Essential Oils/Incense
Cedar: Protects and enhances your assets
Cinnamon: Encourages financial gain from a successful career or business endeavor
Clove: Stimulates financial growth
Vervain: Helps your financial goals materialize
Herbs and Spices
Cinnamon: Revs up the spell's power
Dill (seed or weed): Attracts good fortune
Parsley: Encourages prosperity and success
Spearmint: One of the most popular, all-purpose money herbs

SPELL TO CREATE A PROSPERITY CONSCIOUSNESS

Before you can attract wealth, you have to feel you are worthy of it. Many of us have been taught to believe we don't deserve prosperity, but those ideas can hinder your ability to achieve financial security. This spell helps you rewrite and revise old, outworn beliefs—see Chapter 5 for information about writing affirmations correctly.

INGREDIENTS/TOOLS:
- 14 green candles
- 1 empty glass container
- An affirmation

BEST TIME TO PERFORM THE SPELL:
- On the new moon

Purchase 14 green candles scented with pine or cedar essential oils. Votives and tea light candles are good to use for this spell. On the night of the new moon, light one of the candles at your altar or special place. While it's burning, say your affirmation aloud and feel its truth. After 5 minutes, extinguish the candle and rub your hands in the smoke. Waft the smoke toward your face, your body, your clothes. Hold your palms to your nose and inhale the scent. Remember the fragrance, and associate it with abundance, prosperity, and your new belief. Set the candle aside.

Repeat this ritual each day for the next 13 days, using a new candle each time. Set each spent candle next to its predecessor at the back of your altar. On the night of the full moon, after you have burned the fourteenth candle, light all fourteen again and let them finish burning down completely. Then pour the melted wax left over from all the candles into a glass container, forming a new candle. This new candle symbolizes your new belief about prosperity. Once the wax has solidified, bury it, symbolically planting it in the ground to make your wealth grow. If you prefer, mold the wax from these other candles around a new wick and burn it to attract abundance.

The Modern Witchcraft Spell Book

SPELL TO ATTRACT PROSPERITY

This spell can be used for any kind of prosperity, but it works best for the fullness of inner peace, the source of all true prosperity. When you truly believe you deserve prosperity, it comes to you effortlessly. Sage is a good herb for getting rid of negativity and cinnamon is excellent for boosting your creativity. Green, as you know, represents money and growth.

INGREDIENTS/TOOLS:
- 1 green candle
- 1 cauldron, or a fireproof ceramic or copper bowl
- 1 sprig of sage
- Matches or a lighter
- A pinch of cinnamon

BEST TIME TO PERFORM THIS SPELL:
- On the new moon

On the night of the new moon, put the green candle in your cauldron or bowl, along with the sage. Light them both. Sprinkle cinnamon into the flame, as you say: "I embrace prosperity and inner peace." Repeat these words and keep sprinkling cinnamon into the flame, until the cinnamon is gone. Let the candle and the sage burn down, then bury the remains in your yard or another place that holds meaning for you.

The Color of Money

In some countries, green is the color of paper money; therefore, your mind automatically makes a connection between green and wealth. If you live in a country where a different color appears on your currency, use that color to symbolize money instead. Gold and silver, the colors of precious metals, are good choices, too.

FENG SHUI WEALTH SPELL

In the ancient Chinese magickal system known as feng shui, red and purple are considered lucky colors. Plants symbolize growth. This spell combines the two symbols to attract wealth.

INGREDIENTS/TOOLS:
- 1 plant with red or purple flowers

BEST TIME TO PERFORM THE SPELL:
- During the waxing moon

Stand at the door you use most often when going in and out of your home, facing inside. Locate the farthest left-hand corner of your home, from your vantage point. That's what's known as your wealth sector. Put the plant in that area to make your wealth grow. Water, feed, and care for the plant with loving kindness. Talk to it. Send it good thoughts. Play classical music for it to enjoy (it may dance even if you can't see it). As you tend the plant and watch it grow, you'll notice your fortune improves, too.

CAULDRON MANIFESTATION SPELL

Wishes don't always materialize overnight—some take a while to develop. Try not to get discouraged and remember that everything happens in its own good time. While you're waiting, cast this spell to nurture your wish and bring it to fruition.

INGREDIENTS/TOOLS:
- 1 sheet of paper
- Scissors
- 1 pen or pencil
- 1 cauldron (or other bowl-shaped container)
- A pinch of powdered ginger
- 1 capsule or tablet blessed thistle
- 1 green cloth

- The day after the new moon

Cut the sheet of paper into 12 strips. On one strip write your wish in the form of an affirmation (see Chapter 5). Fold the paper strip three times and put it in the cauldron. Sprinkle a little powdered ginger in the cauldron (to speed up results) and a little blessed thistle (to help your goal manifest). You can purchase blessed thistle herbal supplements online, in health food stores, and in some supermarkets. Open a capsule or grind a tablet into powder, then add it to the cauldron. Cover the cauldron with the green cloth.

Allow the spell to "simmer" overnight, then in the morning remove the cloth and repeat the spell. Continue in this manner for a total of 12 days. If your wish hasn't materialized by the time of the full moon, take a break during the waning moon period and begin again on the first day of the waxing moon. Don't give up—trust that your wish will indeed manifest when the time is right.

SPELL TO REPLENISH YOUR WEALTH

Traditionally, mint is associated with prosperity and lemon with cleansing. Combine them with pepper to create a powerful spell to replenish your finances. If you've been in a creative slump, your finances are stagnant, or you've hit a dry period, this spell can stimulate prosperity.

INGREDIENTS/TOOLS:

- 1 paring knife
- 1 lemon
- 1 handful fresh mint leaves
- 1 glass bowl
- 3 bay leaves
- 3 peppercorns
- 1 small piece of aventurine
- 1 small piece of tiger's eye

- During the waxing moon, especially on a Thursday or Friday, or when the sun or moon is in Taurus

Slice the lemon and dry the slices in the oven at a low temperature. Sprinkle the mint leaves over the bottom of a glass bowl, then lay the dry lemon slices over the mint. Place the bay leaves on top of the lemons. In the center, position the 3 peppercorns and then set the aventurine and the tiger's eye atop the peppercorns. Hold your hands, palms down, over the bowl and close your eyes. The bowl represents nourishment and fullness. Envision the bowl filled with money—an endless supply that replenishes itself whenever you dip into it. Imagine yourself plucking whatever you need from the bowl—the money actually rises into your hands, as if your palms were magnets. No matter how much you remove, more money flows in to fill the bowl again.

MINT YOUR OWN

Wouldn't it be nice if you could mint your own money? Then you'd never have to worry about having enough. Well now you can. No, we're not talking about counterfeiting. Instead, use magick to make your wealth grow.

Ingredients/Tools:
- 1 likeness of a million-dollar bill
- 1 green ceramic flowerpot
- Potting soil
- Spearmint or peppermint seeds, or a small mint plant
- Water

Best time to perform the spell:
- During the waxing moon, preferably when the sun or moon is in Taurus

Make a likeness of a million-dollar bill—you can draw one or download one from the Internet (even though there aren't any real million-dollar bills, that big number gets your attention). Fold the bill three times and place it in the bottom of the ceramic flowerpot. Fill the pot with soil. Plant the seeds or seedling in the soil and water it.

As you work, repeat this incantation:

"Every day
In every way
Prosperity
Now comes to me."

Set the flowerpot in a spot in what feng shui calls your wealth sector (unless the conditions there aren't favorable for the plant). Continue caring for your mint plant and remember to recite the incantation daily. When you trim the plant, save the leaves and dry them to use in talismans. As the plant grows, so will your finances.

PROSPERITY BREW

This spell uses herbal magick plus the symbolism of growing plants, along with a little help from feng shui to attract prosperity. You can also drink this brew hot or cold, to increase your prosperity consciousness.

INGREDIENTS/TOOLS:
- 1 cup of water
- 1 saucepan
- Fresh, chopped parsley
- Fresh, chopped mint leaves
- 1 wooden spoon
- 1 strainer

BEST TIME TO PERFORM THE SPELL:
- On the new moon

On the night of the new moon, pour a cup of water into a pot and begin heating it on the stove. Put the parsley and mint in the water and say, "I embrace prosperity and open myself to receive abundance of all kinds." Stir the brew with a wooden spoon, making three clockwise circles to charge the mixture. Bring the water to a boil, then turn off the stove and allow the brew to cool. Strain, then pour the water on the plant you placed in your wealth sector (see the Feng Shui Wealth Spell) or use it to water other plants in your home or yard.

No Limits on Wealth

Does performing a prosperity spell take away someone else's prosperity? Not at all! Prosperity and abundance don't have limits—the universe's riches are infinite and available to everyone. These spells might not work, however, if you're attempting to swindle someone out of money or to profit from someone else's loss.

QUICK CASH POTION

Do you need cash in a hurry? This magick potion starts working as soon as you ingest it. You can either brew this potion as a hot tea or enjoy it as a cool drink. If you like, share it with someone else whose intention is linked with your own.

INGREDIENTS/TOOLS:
- 1 paring knife
- Fresh ginger root
- Fresh mint leaves
- Spring water
- Cinnamon
- 1 clear glass or cup (no designs)
- The ace of pentacles from a tarot deck or the ace of diamonds from a regular deck of playing cards

BEST TIME TO PERFORM THE SPELL:
- During the waxing moon, preferably on a Thursday, but in an emergency do the spell as necessary

Chop the ginger and mint leaves very fine—the amount you use is up to you. Sprinkle them in the spring water, then add a dash of cinnamon.

If you wish, heat the water to make a tea (but don't let it boil). Pour the herb water in a clear glass or cup. Lay the card face up on your altar, table, or countertop and set the glass of water on top of it. Leave it for 5 minutes to allow the image on the card to imprint the water with its vibrations, then drink the tea.

SPELL TO CURB SPENDING

Is money going out faster than it's coming in? This spell taps the magick of feng shui to slow your cash outflow and help you get a handle on spending.

INGREDIENTS/TOOLS:
- All your credit cards
- 1 black envelope
- A few drops pine essential oil
- 1 piece of tumbled hematite
- 1 small piece of tumbled onyx
- Your wallet or purse
- 1 large stone (one that weighs at least a pound or two)

BEST TIME TO PERFORM THE SPELL:
- During the waning moon, preferably on a Saturday, or when the sun or moon is in Capricorn

Sort through your credit cards and place the ones you don't need or don't use regularly—as many as possible—in the black envelope. (You might consider canceling some of them while you're at it.) Next, dab a little essential oil on each of the stones. After the oil dries, slip the hematite in your wallet or purse—each time you reach for your cash, touch the stone to remind you of your intention.

Stash the envelope containing your credit cards in a safe spot and set the piece of onyx on it to symbolically hold down spending. Finally, place the large stone in the wealth sector of your home. To locate this, stand at the entrance to your home (the one you use most often, not necessarily the front door) with your back to the door, so you're looking inside. The farthest left-hand corner is the wealth sector.

Additional suggestion: If you want to cut back on business expenditures, you could put another piece of hematite or onyx in your cash register or safe, and another large stone in the wealth sector at your place of business.

AMULET TO WARD OFF CREDITORS

Are annoying phone calls and angry demand letters from creditors driving you nuts? Although you may be doing the best you can, collection agencies can be as persistent as pit bulls. This amulet helps to ward off creditors the way ancient amulets repelled evil spirits.

INGREDIENTS/TOOLS:
- 1 image of a bear
- The rune *Eihwaz*
- 1 small piece of turquoise
- Dried basil leaves
- Dried fennel
- Dried parsley
- 1 black drawstring pouch, made of cloth or leather

BEST TIME TO PERFORM THE SPELL:
- During the waning moon, preferably on a Saturday, or when the sun or moon is in Capricorn

Gather all the ingredients listed. The image of a bear could be a magazine picture, a small figurine, a jewelry charm, or a drawing you sketch yourself. The rune *Eihwaz*, which means "defense," could be a piece of stone, ceramic, wood, or metal with the symbol carved or painted on it. (It looks a bit like a reversed Z tilted slightly.) Wash the turquoise with mild soap and water, then pat it dry.

Place the herbs, rune, and piece of turquoise in the pouch. Then hold the image of the bear in your hand and gaze at it. The bear represents protection and fortitude. Ask the spirit bear, symbolized by this image, to defend you against harassment and to give you the strength to "bear up" under the challenge you are facing. Add the bear to your pouch and close the pouch. Wear the amulet or carry it with you while you continue resolving your financial issues.

A FETISH TO FIGHT BAD LUCK

We've all run into streaks of bad luck. Fashion a few of these fetishes, and use them to help disperse negative energy that can wreak havoc with your finances.

INGREDIENTS/TOOLS:
- 3 pennies (or other coins of small denomination)
- 3 pieces of green, gold, or silver cloth
- 3 pieces of white string or ribbon

BEST TIME TO PERFORM THE SPELL:
- Anytime

Place the pennies into the pieces of cloth, then tie them with the string or ribbon. As you tie the knots, recite this incantation:

"In luck I trust,
In luck I believe,
Within this bundle,
Abundance weave!"

To activate the fetish, take it to a remote location away from water or trees, and bury it in the ground. Say aloud:

"Bad fortune's come,
But not to stay.
I command it now
To turn away."

Turn away from the place where you've buried the bundle and don't look back. Visualize leaving behind all negative energy that hindered you in the past.

KEEP IT COMING PROSPERITY CIRCLE

Even if your present financial situation is sound, you can't predict what the future may bring. This spell ensures that prosperity will continue flowing toward you and that you'll always have more than enough money to cover your expenses.

INGREDIENTS/TOOLS:
- 9 small jars (baby food jars are perfect)
- 1 piece of paper
- 1 pen that writes green, gold, or silver ink
- Coins (any denomination)

BEST TIME TO PERFORM THE SPELL:
- Daily, beginning during the waxing moon

Choose a spot in your home or workplace where you can leave the jars in position permanently, where they won't be disturbed. Arrange the empty jars in a circle. On the piece of paper write the following affirmation: "I now have plenty of money for everything I need and desire and plenty to share with others." Lay the paper in the center of the circle of jars and put a coin on top to secure it. Then beginning at the east, work in a clockwise direction and drop one coin in each jar. Repeat the affirmation aloud each time you place a coin in a jar.

The next day add another coin to each jar, again starting at the east and working in a clockwise direction. Continue in this manner, adding one coin per day to each jar. When all the jars are full, remove the coins and donate the money to your favorite charity. As you give the money away, repeat the following affirmation three times: "I offer this money with love and gratitude. I now receive my tenfold return, with good to all concerned."

Start filling the jars again, in the same manner as before. Continue performing this spell and sharing your wealth indefinitely, in order to keep prosperity coming your way forever.

WHEEL OF FORTUNE

Does it seem that you never have enough money left over after paying the bills to buy anything extra? You're just scraping by. Will you ever manage to get ahead so you can treat yourself to a few luxuries? This spell helps you attract good fortune and acquire the objects you desire.

INGREDIENTS/TOOLS:
- Pictures of things you'd like to have
- Scissors
- 1 sheet of heavy paper or poster board
- Glue, paste, or tape
- The Wheel of Fortune card from a tarot deck you don't use for readings

BEST TIME TO PERFORM THE SPELL:
- During the waxing moon, preferably on a Thursday

Cut out pictures from magazines or catalogs, or download images from the Internet that depict the goodies you covet: a new car, a designer wardrobe, jewelry, the latest computer—whatever strikes your fancy. Cut the paper into the shape of a circle or wheel. Glue or tape the Wheel of Fortune card in the center of the paper circle. Arrange the pictures you've selected around the tarot card and fasten them to the paper. As you work, imagine all these wonderful things belonging to you. See yourself driving that new car or donning those diamonds. Make your visions as real as possible.

Display your "wheel of fortune" in a place where you will see it often. You might want to put it in what feng shui calls the wealth sector of your home or workplace. To locate this, stand at the entrance to your home or workplace—the one you use most often, not necessarily the front door—with your back to the door, so you're looking inside. The farthest left-hand corner is the wealth sector. Each time you look at your collage, you'll reinforce your intention to draw abundance into your life.

MONEY TREE SPELL

Money may not grow on trees, but you can tap the growth symbolism inherent in trees to increase your income. Whether you need cash to cover an unexpected expense, seek extra money for something special, or just want to improve your financial status, this spell helps you attract abundance of all kinds.

INGREDIENTS/TOOLS:
- Gold and/or silver ribbons
- Small charms, earrings, beads, crystals, and/or other ornaments
- Bells or wind chimes

BEST TIME TO PERFORM THE SPELL:
- During the waxing moon, preferably on a Thursday or Friday, or when the sun or moon is in Taurus

Tie the ribbons loosely on the branches of a favorite tree. The tree can be one on your own property or in a place that's special to you. Hang the other adornments on the branches as well. These objects represent gifts or offerings to the nature spirits, in return for their assistance in bringing you wealth. The earth elementals called gnomes really like bling and will appreciate these trinkets. As you attach each item, state your intention aloud and ask the nature spirits to help you acquire what you desire. When you've finished, thank the tree and the nature spirits.

PROSPERITY FRUIT SALAD

This seasonal breakfast or dessert combines fruits associated with prosperity and abundance. When you eat them, you take their energy into your body, which symbolizes your willingness to accept prosperity into your life. Blend the fruits according to your own taste preferences and your personal associations with them.

INGREDIENTS/TOOLS:
- Fresh pineapple chunks
- Blueberries

- Cherries, pitted and sliced in half
- Grapes, sliced in half, seeds removed
- Apples, diced
- Pears, diced
- 1 glass bowl
- 1 teaspoon lemon juice
- ¼ cup sugar

BEST TIME TO PERFORM THIS SPELL:
- During the waxing moon

Wash, dry, and cut the fruit into bite-sized pieces. Combine the fruit in a bowl. Sprinkle the lemon juice over the fruit. Sprinkle the sugar over the fruit and let sit for 1 hour. Enjoy, while you envision prosperity flowing toward you.

Chapter 11

SPELLS FOR SAFETY AND PROTECTION

Spells to provide protection were among the earliest and most sought-after forms of magick. Hunters, warriors, travelers—and just about everyone else—hoped spells would safeguard them against injuries, illness, robbers, bad luck, natural calamities, and evil in all its many forms. Even in modern times, if you travel to Greece or Turkey you'll likely see "evil eye" amulets everywhere—usually depicted as blue eye-like symbols made of glass or ceramic—hanging in homes, businesses, and cars to ward off dangerous forces. And who among us hasn't thrown salt over his shoulder to protect against bad luck, or crossed herself in the face of adversity, or carried a special object along when starting a journey?

Today, danger lurks all around us, just as it did millennia ago. Even though we may no longer believe that someone will curse us with the "evil eye," we still seek protection from automobile accidents, criminal elements, physical ailments, and other types of harm. The spells in this chapter are designed to protect you (or someone you care about) from adversity. What if you can't find an item that's called for in a spell? The tables included here show which ingredients to substitute if necessary, or if you just want to make a spell more personal.

Steps for Successful Spellcasting

Whenever you cast a spell, remember to use a few tried-and-true measures, as described in Chapter 1. These precautions can help you avoid complications, mix-ups, delays, or disappointments:

1. Remove all distractions.
2. Collect the ingredients and tools you'll use in your spell and cleanse them.
3. Purify and sanctify your space.
4. Quiet your mind.
5. Cast a circle around the area where you'll do your spellworking.
6. Perform the spell.
7. If you've called upon deities or spirits to assist you, thank and release them.
8. Open the circle.
9. Store your tools in a safe place until you need them again.

COLORS TO USE IN PROTECTION SPELLS

To enhance the spells you do for safety and protection, incorporate the colors white or black—although if your aim is to improve your psychic ability for protection, use indigo. The most popular ways to bring in these colors are to burn candles or craft amulet pouches in these colors. You may also want to carry black or white gemstones as amulets, wear black or white clothing while performing protection spells, or add white flower petals to mojo bags, ritual baths, sachets, or potions. Many of the spells in this chapter use these color associations.

INGREDIENTS FOR PROTECTION SPELLS

Gemstones

Amber: Though not really a stone—it's fossilized sap—amber offers protection from physical or nonphysical threats

Bloodstone: Provides physical protection and bolsters courage; the ancients believed it stanched the flow of blood

Onyx: Gives you strength to stand up to your adversaries

Peridot: Repels negative energies and neutralizes toxins

Snowflake obsidian: Provides overall protection

Tourmaline: Shields you from unwanted energies in the environment, such as EMFs

Flowers

Carnation (white): Brings protection and strength

Geranium (white): Helps protect you and your home

Lilac (white): Offers general protection and banishes negative energy

Lily (white): Repels and removes hexes; guards the soul as it journeys into the afterlife

Snapdragon (white): Protects you from illusion or deception; safeguards your home

Essential Oils/Incense

Anise (star): Protects against negative energy

Fennel: Provides physical and psychic protection

Pine: Guards against negativity and evil spirits

Herbs and Spices

Angelica: Use it magickally for protection and purification

Basil: One of the most popular, all-round protection herbs

Caraway (seeds): Protects you and your home from thieves

Comfrey: Provides protection while traveling

Rosemary: Provides safety and clears negative vibes

GEMSTONE NECKLACE FOR A SAFE TRIP

Although statistics show that most accidents happen near home, it's natural to feel a little anxious about your safety when you're going on a long trip. This gemstone amulet is more than a pretty necklace; it also provides protection while you're traveling.

INGREDIENTS/TOOLS:
- Amber beads
- Jade beads
- Turquoise beads
- Bloodstone beads
- Agate beads
- Silver or gold charms in the shape of angels, stars, pentagrams, and so on (optional)
- Jeweler's elastic

BEST TIME TO PERFORM THE SPELL:
- At least 3 days before your trip

Cut a length of jeweler's elastic long enough to wear as a necklace (if you prefer, you can make a bracelet instead). Begin stringing the beads on the jeweler's elastic. You can alternate the beads on a single string or, if you prefer, make three separate strands and twist them together. Add charms that symbolize protection, if you like.

As you work, visualize yourself safe and sound, traveling with ease wherever you go. Imagine a ball of pure white light surrounding you and shielding you from harm. When you've finished, tie a knot in the elastic. As you tie it, say this affirmation aloud: "This necklace keeps me safe and sound at all times and in all situations, now and always." Wear the amulet to protect you when you travel.

HERBAL PROTECTION PILLOW

Are closet monsters and bad dreams preventing you from getting a good night's sleep? Do you keep hearing things go bump in the night? This fragrant protection pillow calms your nerves and helps you relax, so you can stop worrying about unwanted nightly visitors.

INGREDIENTS/TOOLS:
- 2 squares of dark blue cloth, 3" × 3" or larger
- White thread
- 1 needle
- Dried basil leaves
- Fennel seeds
- Rosemary
- Dried parsley
- Lavender flowers
- Lemongrass
- Sage

BEST TIME TO PERFORM THE SPELL:
- On the new moon

Collect the ingredients listed. Sew the squares of blue cloth together on three sides—it's best if you do it by hand, rather than with a sewing machine. After you've finished, fill the casing with the herbs. Sew the fourth side closed to make a tiny pillow. Place the herbal protection pillow under your regular bed pillow. If you prefer, lay the protection pillow beside you so you can smell its soothing scent during the night.

TOTEM ANIMAL SPELL TO PROTECT YOUR HOME

Do you have a totem animal? Totems serve as spirit guardians and helpers—you can call upon them to aid you in times of need. Your totem is an animal, bird, reptile, or insect with which you feel a strong sense of kinship and which, to you, represents protective power. (For more information about totem animals, see Chapter 7 and my book *The Secret Power of Spirit Animals*).

INGREDIENTS/TOOLS:
- 1 image of an animal totem

- Basil leaves
- Bowl (optional)

- 3 days before the new moon, or whenever you feel the need

Select an image of your totem animal—a figurine, drawing, photograph, or image downloaded from the Internet—and place it near your front door. Say aloud, to your animal guardian:

"Protect this home,
High to low,
Fence to fence,
Door to door,
Light to dense,
Roof to floor."

Next, scatter the basil leaves all around the outside of your home. If you live in an apartment, either scatter them around the entire building or, instead, place the leaves in a bowl and set the bowl and your animal image just inside the door to your apartment.

PROTECTION AMULET FOR YOUR HOME

Here's another way to protect your home. You can also do this spell to safeguard your business, car, or other possessions—simply substitute a picture of whatever you intend to protect.

INGREDIENTS/TOOLS:
- 1 white candle
- 1 picture of your house
- 1 silver pentagram
- Dried petals from a white carnation
- 1 ash leaf
- 1 quartz crystal
- 1 piece of white coral

- 1 moonstone
- 1 piece of amber
- 1 white pouch, preferably made of silk
- 1 black ribbon
- Saltwater

- On a Saturday or when the sun or moon is in Capricorn; however, if you feel at risk, do the spell as soon as possible

Set the candle on your altar and light it. Lay the picture of your house on the altar in front of the candle and put the pentagram on it (or draw a pentagram on the back of the picture). Gaze at the picture and, at the same time, envision a sphere of white light completely surrounding your home. Say aloud,

"My home is now protected
At all times,
In all situations,
Always and all ways."

Place the flower petals, ash leaf, crystal, coral, moonstone, and amber in the white silk pouch. Add the picture of your home and the pentagram. Tie the pouch closed with the ribbon, making 8 knots. With each knot, repeat your affirmation while you hold the vision of your home, surrounded by white light, in your mind's eye. After you've finished, sprinkle the amulet with saltwater to charge it. Extinguish the candle. Hang the amulet inside the front door to safeguard your home and your possessions.

SPELL TO BANISH SPIRITS FROM YOUR HOME

Are unidentified spirits or bad vibes invading your home? Do you sense tension or animosity from neighbors, previous residents, or maybe even ghosts? This spell banishes unwanted energies and prevents "psychic intruders" from coming back.

INGREDIENTS/TOOLS:

- 1 stick of sage incense or a sage wand
- Matches or a lighter
- 1 large pot
- 2 or more quarts of water
- 1 large bunch of fresh basil
- 1 pitcher

BEST TIME TO PERFORM THE SPELL:

- On a Saturday at dusk, preferably when the sun or moon is in Cancer or Capricorn

Light the sage incense or wand and allow the smoke to waft through your home. Walk through each room, letting the smoke clear the air. Call out to the unwanted energies and order them: "Be gone." After you've finished, pour the water in the pot and heat it. Add the basil and let it simmer for 10 minutes. Allow the brew to cool. Strain the basil out and pour the water into a pitcher. Set the basil aside to dry; save it to use in other spells. Take the pitcher of basil-infused water outside and pour it on the ground near your front door, drawing a pentagram with the liquid. As you mark the ground with the pentagram, say this incantation aloud:

"Harmful spirits stay away.
Ill intentions keep at bay.
My home is safe all night and day."

Repeat the process at your back door (and any other doors that lead into your home).

Spicy Sachet for Protection

A sachet of rosemary, angelica, sage, 3 cloves, and a pinch of salt tied shut with white ribbon is a good all-purpose amulet to hang above a door or to keep in your car for protection.

SEALING OIL

Use this oil to protect any items you choose: your purse, jewelry, car, home, etc. You can even put it on your pet's collar to keep Fluffy or Fido safe.

INGREDIENTS/TOOLS:
- 1 glass jar or bottle
- 3 tablespoons olive oil
- 3 pinches salt
- 1 whole clove
- 1 basil leaf

BEST TIME TO PERFORM THE SPELL:
- As needed

Wash the jar or bottle. Combine all the ingredients in it. Place it in a sunny spot and allow the ingredients to infuse for 3 days. When the magick oil is ready, dip your finger in it and draw a line across or along whatever you are sealing (around a door or window frame, inside the opening of your purse, etc.).

FINANCIAL PROTECTION AMULET

Are rising expenses, bad investments, loss of work, or debts threatening your financial security? This amulet helps to protect your assets and your serenity.

INGREDIENTS/TOOLS:
- 1 black marker
- 1 circle of soft, flexible leather (deerskin is perfect) 8" in diameter
- 1 single-hole paper punch
- 1 leather cord
- Alfalfa
- Small pieces or wood chips of cedar, ash, or pine
- 1 cauldron
- Matches or a lighter
- 1 small piece of aventurine
- 1 small piece of onyx

- On a Saturday, or when the sun or moon is in Capricorn

Choose a place where you can burn a small fire safely. With the marker, draw a pentagram on the inside center of the leather circle. With the paper punch, make small holes around the outside of the leather circle, large enough that you can slide the cord through them. Thread the cord through the holes. Pull up the outer edges of the circle, tightening the cord to form a pouch (with the pentagram inside on the bottom).

Put the alfalfa and wood chips in the cauldron. Light them and let them burn completely. Allow the ashes to cool. Pour the ashes into the pouch, then add the gemstones. Close the pouch and tie 3 knots in the cord.

Place the amulet in the wealth sector of your home or business. To locate this, stand at the entrance to your home (the one you use most often, not necessarily the front door) with your back to the door, so you're looking inside. The farthest left-hand corner is the wealth sector. If you prefer, put the amulet in your safe, cash register, or purse to safeguard your finances.

PROTECTION BATH

This relaxing spell is good to do at night, before you go to bed, to remove any bad vibes you may have picked up during the day. It cleanses your body, mind, and spirit of unwanted energies and safeguards you while your spirit travels during sleep.

Ingredients/Tools:
- 4 white candles in unbreakable holders
- Matches or a lighter
- 4 clear quartz crystals
- A bathtub full of comfortably hot water
- ½ cup Epsom salts
- A few drops of lavender essential oil
- A few drops of fennel, basil, or cedar oil—or a combination

- Every night, or as often as possible

Set the candles in their holders at the corners of your bathtub and light them. Place one quartz crystal beside each candle. Fill the tub with water while you pour in the Epsom salts. Add the essential oils. Soak in the fragrant, soothing water for as long as you wish, while you envision yourself cleansed and cleared of all negative, harmful, and/or unbalanced energies. See yourself surrounded by a bubble of white light that will continue to protect you even after you leave the bath.

Extinguish the candles and get out of the water; empty the tub. You can carry the crystals with you throughout the day, or leave them on the corners of the tub—your choice.

BRAVE HEART LOTION

If you suffer from stage fright or feel uncomfortable speaking in front of a group of people, whip up a batch of this magick lotion and use it to boost your confidence. You can also use it if you feel nervous about a job interview, important meeting, or big game.

Ingredients/Tools:
- 1 small carnelian, garnet, or ruby
- 1 glass jar or bottle, preferably amber-colored, with a lid or stopper
- 4 ounces of almond oil
- 3 drops of fennel essential oil
- 3 drops of cedar essential oil
- ¼ teaspoon dried basil leaves

Best time to perform the spell:
- Several days before your public appearance, preferably on a Tuesday or Sunday; if you don't have that much time, do the spell as needed

Wash the gemstone and the bottle/jar with mild soap and water. Pour the almond oil into the bottle/jar. Add the essential oils and inhale the fragrance, allowing it to invigorate your mind. Crumble the basil leaves very fine and add them to the oil. Add the gemstone. Cap the bottle/jar and shake it three times to blend and charge the ingredients.

Each morning, pour a little of the magick oil into your palm and dip your index finger in it. Then rub the oil on your skin at your heart center. Feel it strengthening your confidence. Take several slow, deep breaths, inhaling the warm, spicy scent, letting it strengthen and vitalize you. Repeat each morning until your fear diminishes. Rub a little extra on your chest immediately before you must face your audience. On with the show!

OIL TO GUARD AGAINST SECRET ENEMIES

You may not realize that someone is working against your best interests, so consider making and using this protection oil regularly. If you do suspect someone is out to get you, this magick oil heightens your strength and helps increase your insight so you can protect yourself before the enemy can strike.

INGREDIENTS/TOOLS:
- 1 glass jar or bottle with a tight-sealing lid
- 3 cloves
- 1 small piece of hematite
- A pinch of salt
- 3 ounces of olive oil

BEST TIME TO PERFORM THE SPELL:
- Whenever you need it, but preferably on a Tuesday or Saturday

Wash the bottle, then place the cloves in the bottle one by one as you visualize the bottle filling with white light. Add the hematite, visualizing the silvery color of the stone weaving and swirling through the white light. Add the salt, and visualize the silver and white light growing brighter. Carefully pour the olive oil into the jar or bottle over the contents, then cap the bottle tightly. Shake it three times to blend and charge the ingredients.

Open the jar or bottle and dip your finger in the oil. Draw a pentagram with the oil on your third eye (the brow chakra) and on the center of your chest (your heart chakra). If you wish, draw additional pentagrams on your other chakras for added protection.

SAFETY SHIELD FOR YOUR CAR

Approximately 2 million people are injured in vehicular accidents each year in the United States (and nearly a quarter of all accidents involve cell phone use). That's a good reason to create this magick safety shield to protect you and your car from harm.

INGREDIENTS/TOOLS:
- 1 nail, nail file, small knife, or other sharp tool
- 1 black candle
- 1 candleholder
- Matches or a lighter
- 1 piece of white paper
- 1 pen that writes black ink

BEST TIME TO PERFORM THE SPELL:
- As needed, but preferably on a Thursday or Saturday

Use the nail or other tool to engrave a pentagram into the candle's wax. Fit the candle in its holder, set it on your altar or another surface, and light the candle. On the piece of paper, draw a circle and write, "I am safe" inside the circle. If you like, add symbols, words, or other images that represent safety to you. You could even draw a picture of your car or write your license plate number on the paper. Drip a bit of melted candle wax on each corner of the paper. Use the nail or other tool to inscribe a pentagram in the warm wax. Extinguish the candle and place the safety shield in your car's glove compartment or affix it to your dashboard. (And don't use your cell phone to text or talk while driving!)

POTION TO PROTECT A LOVED ONE

Are you worried about a friend or loved one's safety? This magick potion protects someone else from harm. However, before you do this spell, ask the other person—either directly or psychically—if it's okay for you to use magick to help him or her, so you don't interfere with another's free will.

INGREDIENTS/TOOLS:
- 1 clear glass bottle with a lid or stopper
- 1 small clear quartz crystal
- Black paint or nail polish
- Water
- 1 kettle or pot
- Dried comfrey or comfrey tea bags

BEST TIME TO PERFORM THE SPELL:
- On a Monday, or when the sun or moon is in Cancer

Wash the bottle and the crystal with mild soap and water, then let them dry. Paint a pentagram on the side of the bottle. Heat the water in a kettle or pot and add the comfrey to it to make a tea (you can purchase comfrey tea bags in health food stores and many supermarkets). Allow it to steep for several minutes, then let it cool. Pour the tea into the bottle. Add the quartz crystal. Put the lid or stopper on the bottle and shake it three times to charge it. Let the potion sit overnight, preferably where the moon can shine on it.

Remove the crystal and give the protection potion to your friend or loved one. If you're afraid this person will think you're weird, you can transfer the tea into another container *sans* pentagram—the tea will retain the imprint of the symbol. Instruct the person to drink a little each day. Additional suggestion: While you're at it, brew some for yourself, too.

QUICK AND EASY FLYING SPELL

This spell requires no tools—just your imagination—and you can do it in a minute or so, right before your plane taxis into position for takeoff. Close your eyes and breathe slowly and deeply. Envision a cocoon of pure white light surrounding the entire plane from nose to tail and out to the tips of the wings. See the light swirling around the plane in a clockwise direction, forming a protective barrier against the elements. Mentally repeat the following affirmation three times: "I now enjoy a comfortable trip and arrive safely at [name of destination airport]." Visualize the plane traveling through the sky and landing safely on the runway at your final destination.

STRENGTH AND SAFETY SOUP

Make this delicious recipe during those times when you feel you need a little extra protection or think you may be coming down with a cold. Garlic and onions are the key ingredients. Romans used garlic for strength, and many people valued it for its protective properties (not just against vampires). Egyptians used onions to keep away harmful spirits and fed onions to their slaves to ensure vitality. This recipe also relies on the number four for its stabilizing, earthy influence.

INGREDIENTS/TOOLS:

- 1 large Spanish onion
- 1 large red onion
- 1 bundle green onions
- 1 white onion
- Frying pan
- 1 tablespoon butter
- 4 small cloves garlic, peeled and crushed
- 4 sticks celery, diced (optional)
- Large saucepan
- 2 cups beef stock
- 2 cups chicken stock
- 2 cups water
- 1 tablespoon Worcestershire sauce (or to taste)
- Croutons and grated cheese (for garnish, optional)

Slice the onions and sauté them in a frying pan with the butter and garlic, until golden brown. For a heartier broth, add the celery and fry it with the onions. Magickally, celery enhances your psychic sight and sense of inner peace. Stir the vegetables counterclockwise as they cook to banish negative energies. Say aloud:

"Onions for health,
And to keep harm at bay,
Garlic for safety
All through the day!"

Keep repeating the incantation until the onions are done. Transfer the onion mixture into a large saucepan, then add the stock, water, and Worcestershire sauce. Cook this mixture down over medium-low heat until it is reduced by 2 cups. Serve the soup with croutons and fresh grated cheese, if desired. Visualize your body being filled with white light as you eat it. You may want to share your magick soup with friends or loved ones.

GUARDIAN ANGEL RITUAL

Numerous polls conducted by Associated Press, AOL, Gallup, and others have found that nearly 80 percent of Americans believe in angels. Here's a way to request angelic assistance and protection. With this ritual you call upon Raphael, Michael, Gabriel, and Uriel. Perform this ritual by itself to petition their aid, or do it in conjunction with other spells. You can also do it with other people, if you choose—just make sure you and your companions are in agreement about your beliefs and intentions.

INGREDIENTS/TOOLS:
- 1 yellow votive candle
- 1 red votive candle
- 1 blue votive candle
- 1 green votive candle
- Matches or a lighter

• Anytime

Stand facing east and set the yellow candle on the ground (or floor) in front of you, where it can burn safely. Light the candle and say aloud:

"Archangel Raphael, Guardian of the East,
Come and be with me in this sacred space.
I request your protection and guidance
In all I do, now and always."

Move clockwise until you are facing south, and set the red candle on the ground (or floor) in front of you. Light the candle and say aloud:

"Archangel Michael, Guardian of the South,
Come and be with me in this sacred space.
I request your protection and guidance
In all I do, now and always."

Move clockwise until you are facing west, and set the blue candle on the ground (or floor) in front of you. Light the candle and say aloud:

"Archangel Gabriel, Guardian of the West,
Come and be with me in this sacred space.
I request your protection and guidance
In all I do, now and always."

Move clockwise until you are facing north, and set the green candle on the ground (or floor) in front of you. Light the candle and say aloud:

"Archangel Uriel, Guardian of the North,
Come and be with me in this sacred space.
I request your protection and guidance
In all I do, now and always."

Move to the center of the circle you've cast. Close your eyes and envision the four archangels standing around you, like sentries protecting you from harm. Feel their power flowing into you, filling you with strength and confidence. Remain in the center of the circle for as long as you wish. If you like, you can perform another spell or ritual now, under the watchful guard of the archangels. When you are ready, release the archangels and open the circle in the following manner.

Go to the east and stand facing outward. Say aloud:

"Archangel Raphael, Guardian of the East,
I thank you for your presence here this night (or day).
Please continue to guide and protect me always and all ways,
Even after you return to your home in the heavens.
Hail, farewell, and blessed be."

Extinguish the yellow candle. Move counterclockwise to the north and stand facing outward. Say aloud:

"Archangel Uriel, Guardian of the North,
I thank you for your presence here this night (or day).
Please continue to guide and protect me always and all ways,
Even after you return to your home in the heavens.
Hail, farewell, and blessed be."

Extinguish the green candle. Go to the west and stand facing outward. Say aloud:

"Archangel Gabriel, Guardian of the West,
I thank you for your presence here this night (or day).
Please continue to guide and protect me always and all ways,
Even after you return to your home in the heavens.
Hail, farewell, and blessed be."

Extinguish the blue candle. Go to the south and stand facing outward. Say aloud:

"Archangel Michael, Guardian of the South,
I thank you for your presence here this night (or day).
Please continue to guide and protect me always and all ways,
Even after you return to your home in the heavens.
Hail, farewell, and blessed be."

Extinguish the red candle. Additional suggestion: You can substitute this longer and more intricate circle-casting ritual for the basic one described in Chapter 3, if you choose.

Chapter 12

SPELLS FOR PERSONAL AND PROFESSIONAL SUCCESS

Because your mind is the architect of your reality, it's inevitable that your thoughts about yourself will generate material conditions that correspond to your ideas. Your life is your mirror. What you see is a reflection of what you believe about yourself. As you evaluate your personal and professional success, look at your entire life situation: your finances, your job, your relationships, your position in your community, and your health. If you aren't happy with your situation, you can change it by changing your perceptions of yourself.

Remember, nobody else gets to decide whether you're worthy of success. Only you do. Consider this quote from Eleanor Roosevelt: "No one can make you feel inferior without your consent." Nor can anyone else limit your personal power without your consent.

The spells in this chapter cover a number of different factors that pertain to success in all areas of life, because really, all areas are connected.

Instead of only aiming for fame and fortune, these spells help you connect with your own power and correct circumstances that may be sabotaging your success. The Spell to Release Negativity, for instance, clears obstacles to success—which may be necessary before you can start attracting the good things and conditions you seek.

Steps for Successful Spellcasting

Whenever you cast a spell, remember to use a few tried-and-true measures, as described in Chapter 1. These precautions can help you avoid complications, mix-ups, delays, or disappointments:

1. Remove all distractions.
2. Collect the ingredients and tools you'll use in your spell and cleanse them.
3. Purify and sanctify your space.
4. Quiet your mind.
5. Cast a circle around the area where you'll do your spellworking.
6. Perform the spell.
7. If you've called upon deities or spirits to assist you, thank and release them.
8. Open the circle.
9. Store your tools in a safe place until you need them again.

COLORS TO USE IN SPELLS FOR SUCCESS

To enhance the spells you do for success, incorporate the colors yellow, gold, and/or orange into your workings. If your aim is to also attract money, you can include green and/or silver. The most popular ways to bring in these colors are to burn candles or craft talisman pouches in these colors. You may also want to carry gemstones in these colors as talismans, or wear yellow, gold, or orange clothing while performing protection spells. Add flower petals that remind you of the sun to mojo bags, ritual baths, sachets, or potions. Many of the spells in this chapter use these color associations.

INGREDIENTS FOR SUCCESS SPELLS

Gemstones

Hematite: Deflects negativity, encourages determination, and promotes justice in legal matters

Onyx: Gives you strength to stand up to your adversaries

Star sapphire: Strengthens hope and clarity of purpose

Topaz: Increases confidence and courage; attracts fame and financial success

Flowers

Clover: Attracts good luck

Iris: The iris's three petals are said to symbolize faith, wisdom, and valor—qualities necessary to success

Lily of the valley: Enhances concentration and mental ability

Marigold: Encourages recognition; brings success in legal matters

Essential Oils/Incense

Cedar: Encourages prosperity and protects against adversaries

Cinnamon: Speeds career success and wealth

Patchouli: Stimulates enthusiasm and success in any endeavor

Sandalwood: Aids mental ability; facilitates guidance and assistance from higher sources

Herbs and Spices

Allspice: Encourages prosperity and good luck

Bay (bay laurel): Used to crown the victor of games in ancient Rome; it enhances success and wisdom

Nettle: Mitigates thorny situations and shows you how to handle problems

Nutmeg: Brings success in financial ventures

SPELL TO RELEASE NEGATIVITY

According to the Law of Attraction, you draw circumstances to you that align with your thoughts and feelings. That means if you've got a negative attitude, you're probably going to attract negative situations and people. Want to turn things around? Swap that bad attitude for a positive one.

INGREDIENTS/TOOLS:
- 1 piece of white paper
- 1 pen that writes blue ink
- White carnations in a clear glass container
- Matches or a lighter

BEST TIME TO PERFORM THIS SPELL:
- During the waning moon

If you encounter a bad situation, this spell breaks the destructive cycle of negativity and restores peace. You may not be able to change what has happened, but you can alter your perspective about it, which can soften the impact. Letting go of negative thoughts and feelings allows fortunate, happier ones to come into your life.

Write the following intention on the paper:

"I now release [name the situation]
And create new, positive energy to carry me forward.
I trust this is for my highest good
And affirm my commitment to this new path."

Place the paper beneath the vase of flowers. Leave it there until the flowers wilt. When you throw out the flowers, burn the paper to complete the releasing process.

POINT OF POWER SPELL

With this spell, you affirm that your point of power is in the present, the "now." At this very moment you can start creating the circumstances you desire—it's your launching pad for the rest of your life. So, get busy!

INGREDIENTS/TOOLS:
- 1 vase of yellow flowers
- 1 piece of turquoise
- 1 green candle
- 1 purple candle
- Matches or a lighter

BEST TIME TO PERFORM THE SPELL:
- On a Thursday or Sunday, during a waxing moon

The yellow flowers symbolize self-esteem and optimism. The green candle represents growth and prosperity, and the purple candle signifies wisdom and power. Turquoise attracts abundance, success, and good fortune.

Place the plant and gemstone on your altar, between the 2 candles. Light the candles and say aloud:

"My point of power,
Like these flowers,
Some way, somehow
Lies in the now."

Extinguish the candles. Carry the gemstone in your pocket or purse to reinforce your sense of personal power. Leave the flowers on your altar until they wither, then collect the petals and dry them for use in future spells.

SIMPLE SPELL TO ATTRACT GOOD THINGS

This simple spell helps you recognize the areas in your life that are rich and satisfying. According to the Law of Attraction, if you perceive yourself as needy, you'll lack things. By counting your blessings and being grateful, you attract more of the same. Like attracts like, as the saying goes.

INGREDIENTS/TOOLS:
- 1 index card
- 1 pen that writes gold or silver ink

BEST TIME TO PERFORM THE SPELL:
- During the waxing moon, preferably on a Sunday, Thursday, or Friday

Write "thank you" on the index card—write it again and again, until you've filled the card. As you write, think about the many things you have to be thankful for. Put the card in a place where you will see it often, such as on your refrigerator, your desk, or your bathroom mirror. Each time you see it, pause and say, "Thank you for [name a blessing]." Give thanks for the little things. Lots of people think only the big things count. We often forget that the big things are made up of the little things. Say thanks for the song that you heard on the radio that made you remember a special day from your childhood. Say thanks for the pouring rain that nourishes your garden. Say thanks for the crossing guard who works near your child's school. Your attitude of gratitude will bring more blessings into your life.

SPELL TO RELEASE PERFECTIONISM

Yes, you read that right. By clinging to the belief that you have to be perfect, you automatically set yourself up to fall short. Instead, do the best you can—and do this spell to release any lingering guilt.

INGREDIENTS/TOOLS:
- 1 piece of vellum or paper
- 1 pen

BEST TIME TO PERFORM THIS SPELL:
- During the waning moon, at sunset

Design an official-looking certificate. On it, write the following:

"I hereby authorize [your name] to be imperfect."

Sign your name. Keep the certificate somewhere safe. Take it out and look at it when you feel guilty for not being a superhero in your daily life.

RAISE YOUR FLAG

This spell lets you "announce" yourself and your goal to the world. Like Buddhist prayer flags, this practice taps the power of the wind to carry your message far and wide.

INGREDIENTS/TOOLS:
- 1 piece of yellow or orange cloth at least 8" × 8" square
- 1 waterproof marker

BEST TIME TO PERFORM THE SPELL:
- During the waxing moon, especially when the sun or moon is in Gemini or Sagittarius, on a Wednesday, at midday

Write your name on the cloth with the marker. Under your name, write an affirmation that states what you wish to achieve. Remember to state your intention in the present tense, and in a positive way (see Chapter 5 for more information). You can add images that symbolize your objective, if you like. (If you have more than one objective, create a different flag for each one.) When you're finished, hang the flag where the wind will make it flutter: a clothesline, flagpole, fence, etc. If your goals change, or the cloth starts looking bedraggled, make another flag to replace it.

SPELL TO BEAT OUT THE COMPETITION

When competition gets brisk or you fear an adversary wants to nudge you out of the picture, remember you have a secret weapon: magick. This spell helps you rise above the rest of the pack and keeps infringers from gaining a foothold.

- Polymer clay
- 1 large needle
- Jewelry elastic
- 1 nonstick baking tray

BEST TIME TO PERFORM THE SPELL:

- On a Tuesday, or when the sun or moon is in Aries

Have you ever seen animals defend their territory? They usually attack with teeth and claws. This spell takes its cue from them. What animal represents courage and ferocity to you? A lion? Bear? Doberman? Maybe a mythological creature such as a dragon? Shamans and sorcerers might use the actual teeth or claws from a totem animal in order to embody that animal's characteristics. You're going to fabricate "teeth" and "claws" from polymer clay to draw on the same symbolism. Select white or ivory clay to simulate the real thing, or another color if you prefer (who knows what color dragon's teeth are?).

Follow the directions on the package of clay to form lots of pointy teeth and claws, each about an inch or two in length. With the needle, pierce each one at the thicker end, making a hole large enough so the jewelry elastic will fit through it. Arrange the teeth and claws on the baking tray, making sure they don't touch each other. Bake according to instructions on the package.

Cut a piece of jewelry elastic long enough to go over your head. When the teeth and claws have cooked and cooled, string them on the elastic to make a necklace. Tie the elastic in a knot at the back. Wear this warrior's necklace to bolster your own courage, so you can scare off the competition and defend what's yours.

SPELL TO SAVE YOUR JOB

If you fear your job is on the line, try not to worry—that will only make matters worse. Instead, use your time and energy more productively by casting this spell.

- 4 white stones
- Black paint, nail polish, or a black felt-tip marker with permanent ink

BEST TIME TO PERFORM THE SPELL:

- Anytime

Collect 4 white stones. They can all be similar in size and shape or they can be different; the choice is yours. After washing the stones with mild soap and water, allow them to dry in the sun. With the black paint, nail polish, or marker, draw a pentagram on each stone to provide protection and security.

Put 1 stone on the floor in each corner of your cubicle, office, or work area to stabilize your position. As you set each stone in place, say or think this affirmation: "My job here is safe and secure, and all is well."

TALISMAN TO MAKE A GOOD IMPRESSION

Whether you're going for a job interview, giving a presentation, or meeting with an important client, this lucky charm helps you make a good impression. Remember, the key to success is believing in yourself. Enthusiasm is catching—if you're enthusiastic about your abilities and ideas, other people will get excited, too.

INGREDIENTS/TOOLS:

- Sandalwood incense
- Incense burner
- Matches or a lighter
- Red nail polish or red paint
- 1 small brush
- 1 small stone
- 1 piece of paper
- 1 pen
- 1 orange cloth pouch, preferably silk
- Cedar chips
- Cinnamon

- Dried parsley
- 1 yellow ribbon
- Saltwater

- On a Sunday, or when the sun or moon is in Leo

Fit the incense in its burner and light it. Use the nail polish or paint to draw the rune *Inguz*, which looks like two Xs stacked one on top of the other, on the stone. This rune represents new beginnings, fertility, and great power.

While the nail polish or paint is drying, write on the paper what you intend to accomplish. Whom do you wish to impress? What results do you desire from this meeting or appearance? As you write your list of objectives, envision yourself already achieving them. When you've finished, fold the paper so it's small enough to fit into the pouch and say aloud: "This is now accomplished in harmony with Divine Will, my own true will, and for the good of all."

Put the stone, paper, cedar, cinnamon, and parsley into the pouch. Tie the pouch closed with the ribbon, making 3 knots. Hold the image of your success in your mind as you tie the knots. Sprinkle the talisman with saltwater, then hold it in the incense smoke for a few moments to charge the talisman. Carry it in your pocket, purse, or briefcase when you go to your meeting to bring you good luck. Just knowing it's there will increase your self-confidence and help you make a good impression.

SPELL TO OPEN NEW DOORS

If downsizing, outsourcing, or another situation beyond your control has eliminated your job, remember the old saying: When one door closes another one opens. This spell uses the familiar symbolism to bring new opportunities your way.

INGREDIENTS/TOOLS:
- Small bells, one for each door in your home
- 9"-long red ribbons, one for each door in your home

- On the new moon

Tie 1 bell at the end of each ribbon, then tie 1 ribbon to each door in your home. As you work, envision yourself attracting new opportunities. If you already know the job you'd like to have, see yourself performing it. Or, if you prefer, let the universe provide a position that's right for you. Each time you tie a ribbon on a doorknob, say the following affirmation aloud: "I now have a job that's perfect for me in every way."

As you go through the doors in your home daily, you'll constantly be reminded of your intention. The red ribbons represent good luck. The tinkling bells send your request out into the world. Repeat your affirmation every time you open a door, until you land the job you desire.

SPELL TO DRUM UP NEW BUSINESS

During slow periods, you may need to step outside the box to attract new clients/customers and opportunities. Since ancient times, drums have been used as a form of communication. Drumming also breaks up stagnant conditions. This spell helps you get the word out magickally—and it won't cost you a fortune in advertising.

INGREDIENTS/TOOLS:
- 1 drum
- 1 picture, token, or other symbol that represents success in your business
- Something to attach the symbol to the drum (e.g., ribbons or tape)

BEST TIME TO PERFORM THE SPELL:
- On the new moon

Fasten the symbol to the drum, by whatever means you prefer. You may be able to simply slide the image beneath the drum's strings. If you prefer, tie it to the drum with a ribbon of an appropriate color. Or you could even paint the symbol on the drum.

Stand facing east and begin drumming. Imagine you are sending a message to the world, inviting one and all to come patronize your business. If you like, extend the invitation to them verbally, explaining all the good things you have to offer them, as if you were doing a commercial. Visualize people flocking to you and enjoying your products or services. After a few minutes, turn to face south and do the same thing. Keep drumming as you turn to face west, and finally to the north. Continue drumming for as long as you like. Repeat this spell as often as you wish, until you have all the business you can handle.

SPELL TO WIN A DECISION

If an upcoming decision will affect your job, your public image, or a project you're working on, use magick to tip the scales in your favor. This spell puts you in a strong position and ensures that you'll be judged fairly.

INGREDIENTS/TOOLS:
- Cinnamon incense
- Incense burner
- Matches or a lighter
- 1 old-fashioned set of scales or 2 white saucers
- The Judgment card from a tarot deck
- 1 picture of yourself
- 1 image that symbolizes "the other" (e.g., a person, issue, or contest)
- 1 piece of watermelon tourmaline
- 1 gold-colored cloth

BEST TIME TO PERFORM THE SPELL:
- During the waxing moon, or when the sun and/or moon is in Libra

Fit the incense in its burner and light it. Set the scale or the saucers on your altar or another spot where they can remain safely in place until the decision is final. If you're using a scale, lay the Judgment card face up in front of it. If you're using 2 saucers, position them next to each other, about 6" apart, and lay the Judgment card face up between them.

Put the picture of yourself on the right side of the scale or in the right saucer. Put the image that symbolizes "the other" on the left side of the scale or in the left saucer.

Place the piece of tourmaline on the right side of the scale or in the right saucer, along with your picture. If you're using a set of scales, the stone will actually tip it in your favor. If you're using saucers, imagine the tourmaline supporting and strengthening you, giving "weight" to your position and bringing you luck. Allow the incense to finish burning down completely while you visualize the decision being made so that you benefit. See yourself happy and successful, winning the challenge. Cover the spell components with the golden cloth. Leave the spell in place until the decision is final.

FENG SHUI SPELL FOR SUCCESS

The ancient Chinese magickal system known as feng shui associates areas of your home with areas of your life. When you stand at the door you use most often to enter and exit your home, facing in, the section halfway between the farthest right-hand corner and the farthest left-hand corner of your home represents your future, fame, career, and public image.

INGREDIENTS/TOOLS:
- 3 objects that represent success to you
- 1 mirror
- 1 bell

BEST TIME TO PERFORM THE SPELL:
- During the waxing moon

In this sector arrange the three objects you've chosen to represent your success. Position the mirror so it reflects these objects, symbolically doubling their impact. Each day, take a few moments to gaze at these objects. Ring the bell as you do this to activate positive energy in this portion of your home. The sound of the bell also triggers your attention and helps you focus on achieving success.

GEMSTONE TALISMAN FOR SUCCESS

This spell can help you succeed—e.g., land a new job, receive a promotion, win a contest, or get a place on the team. Its power comes from combining the magickal meanings of rune symbols with the energies inherent in gemstones—fueled by your desire.

INGREDIENTS/TOOLS:
- Book or list of rune symbols
- Gold paint or metallic gold nail polish
- 3 gemstones that correspond to your objective (see the table at the beginning of this chapter and in Chapter 4 for suggestions)
- 1 gold pouch
- 1 red ribbon 12" long

BEST TIME TO PERFORM THE SPELL:
- During the waxing moon, preferably when the sun or moon is in Leo

Look through a book or list of rune symbols and select 3 that represent goals, conditions, or outcomes you desire. Paint 1 rune on each of the gemstones. When the paint dries, put all the stones into the pouch and tie it closed with the ribbon. Make 3 knots in the ribbon, one for each stone, and think about the intentions you've chosen. Carry the talisman in your pocket, purse, or backpack. If you prefer, place it in a desk drawer or on your altar.

DRESS FOR SUCCESS

Clothes may not make the man or woman, but how you dress does influence the way people think about you and react to you. The President wouldn't address the nation in a pair of ragged jeans and a T-shirt, would he? If you aspire to a position of authority or prominence, start dressing as if you already have that position—even if your dream hasn't manifested yet. In this way, you not only make a statement to others, you send a message to your subconscious that you expect it to help you achieve your goal.

- Clothing, jewelry, accessories, etc. befitting the position you desire

BEST TIME TO PERFORM THE SPELL:
- Each morning, during the waxing moon, when the sun and/or moon is in Leo, on Samhain Eve (October 31), or on your birthday

Each day before you go out into the world, look in your mirror and affirm that you have already achieved the position you seek. Envision yourself performing the role you desire with great skill and satisfaction. Close your eyes and imagine your aura (the energy field around your body) expanding until it extends at least 1' out from your body in every direction, then envision that aura glowing with radiant golden light. Don't just see this light, feel it tingling all around you, warming you with its power, permeating your entire being. Imagine other people noticing and responding favorably to this golden glow. Now, open your eyes and see the very best in yourself—others will, too.

Chapter 13

HEALTH AND HEALING SPELLS

Our ancestors didn't have the advantage of modern medical procedures and pharmaceuticals, as we do today. Instead, when people became ill they relied on plant-based remedies, magick potions, and healing spells to treat ailments and injuries. In many parts of the world, that's still the case. But even in the United States, herbal medicine, essential oils, and various types of holistic healing are gaining popularity. Doctors also acknowledge that our thoughts and emotions have a lot to do with our physical well-being. Numerous studies show that meditation, visualization, and prayer can have a positive effect on health, too.

To some, that may sound like magick—and perhaps it is. As you already know, harnessing your mental power is the key to spellworking. You also understand that working with the forces of nature—plants, minerals, and so on—and tapping the energies inherent in them can help to bring about the conditions you desire. You're aware, too, that you can call upon spiritual beings to assist you in your spells. So it makes sense that magick spells can influence your health and other people's. In this chapter, you'll find spells to aid a variety of problems. But remember, before you cast a spell for someone else, ask that person (either directly or through psychic communication) if it's okay to use magick to help. That way you won't interfere with his or her free will. Just to be on the safe side, it's a good idea to end a spell with a statement such as: "This is done for the good of all concerned." Of course, spells are not intended to replace professional medical care.

Steps for Successful Spellcasting

Whenever you cast a spell, remember to use a few tried-and-true measures, as described in Chapter 1. These precautions can help you avoid complications, mix-ups, delays, or disappointments:

1. Remove all distractions.
2. Collect the ingredients and tools you'll use in your spell and cleanse them.
3. Purify and sanctify your space.
4. Quiet your mind.
5. Cast a circle around the area where you'll do your spellworking.
6. Perform the spell.
7. If you've called upon deities or spirits to assist you, thank and release them.
8. Open the circle.
9. Store your tools in a safe place until you need them again.

COLORS TO USE IN SPELLS FOR HEALTH AND HEALING

To enhance the spells you do for success, incorporate the colors green and blue into your magickal workings. White signifies purification and protection, so you can use it in healing spells, too. Consider burning candles or crafting talisman/amulet pouches in these colors. You may also want to carry gemstones in these colors as talismans or amulets, and wear green or blue clothing while performing health and healing spells. Add green or blue botanicals to mojo bags, ritual baths, sachets, or potions. Many of the spells in this chapter use these color associations.

INGREDIENTS FOR HEALTH AND HEALING SPELLS

Gemstones

Amethyst: Increases relaxation

Chrysocolla: Eases emotional pain

Citrine: Promotes cleansing and dissolves impurities

Fluorite: Eases stress and stress-related problems

Jade: Encourages good health and longevity

Jasper: Brown jasper supports physical healing; poppy jasper breaks up blockages that prevent energy from circulating through the body

Flowers/Plants

Aloe: Aids burns; soothes stomach and intestinal problems

Calendula: Soothes cuts and skin conditions

Gardenia: Brings tranquility and harmony

Lavender: Calms body, mind, and spirit, and encourages relaxation and sleep

Essential Oils/Incense

Eucalyptus: Relieves congestion and soothes colds

Lavender: Encourages relaxation and sleep

Sweet marjoram: Eases muscle and joint pain/stiffness

Herbs and Spices

Chamomile: Aids stomach problems; eases stress and supports relaxation

Comfrey: Encourages bone health and healing

Ginger: Improves digestion, calms nausea

Peppermint: Aids digestion and heartburn, eases headaches

Yarrow: In a poultice, it helps stanch bleeding

When you do a healing spell, you first clear away the obstruction, disruption, or negative energy that is causing the problem. Then you impart positive energy and harmony to the person seeking aid, to support his or her immune system so the problem doesn't return.

ABRACADABRA

Everybody knows the magick word *Abracadabra*—if you say it aloud, will it make your troubles disappear? Actually, it's better if you write it the way ancient healers did. This spell is thousands of years old, but it's still powerful medicine today.

INGREDIENTS/TOOLS:

- 1 blue candle
- 1 candleholder
- Matches or a lighter
- 1 piece of paper or parchment
- 1 pen or marker

BEST TIME TO PERFORM THE SPELL:

- During the waning moon, preferably when the sun or moon is in Virgo or Pisces

Fit the candle in its holder and light it. On the paper or parchment write the word *Abracadabra* as a descending triangle, like this:

```
ABRACADABRA
ABRACADABR
ABRACADAB
ABRACADA
ABRACAD
ABRACA
ABRAC
ABRA
ABR
AB
A
```

When you've finished, extinguish the candle and open the circle. Place the paper on the afflicted part of your body for a few minutes. Envision the illness or injury being transmitted into the symbol. Then remove the paper and take it outside. Tuck the paper in the cleft of a tree, where it will be exposed to the elements. As the word and the paper perish, your discomfort disappears.

WEIGHT LOSS POTION

If your jeans are getting tight and you're not sure you want to be seen in a swimsuit just now, what can you do to shed those unwanted pounds? This magick potion works at a subconscious level to calm hunger pangs and help you stick to your diet.

INGREDIENTS/TOOLS:
- Spring water
- Unsweetened green apple tea (not spiced apple)
- 1 bright pink ceramic cup
- 1 bright pink candle
- 1 candleholder
- Matches or a lighter

- During the waning moon, preferably on a Saturday or when the sun or moon is in Virgo or Capricorn

When you feel hungry, instead of eating something you shouldn't, brew a pot of green apple tea. Pour the tea into the bright pink cup. Fit the candle into its holder, set it on the dining or kitchen table, and light it. Sit and gaze at the candle while you inhale the refreshing scent of the tea. Drink the cup of tea slowly, keeping your attention focused on the candle. Feel your hunger pangs gradually subside. Repeat as necessary.

PAIN, PAIN GO AWAY

After a stressful day, does your head feel like someone is tightening a clamp around it? The key to this spell is detaching yourself from the pain, rather than resisting it.

INGREDIENTS/TOOLS:
- None

BEST TIME TO PERFORM THE SPELL:
- Anytime

Sit in a comfortable place. Close your eyes. Acknowledge the presence of the pain, rather than fighting it. Don't identify with it, however. Try to envision it as something that's not a part of you. Mentally step back, so that your awareness is slightly above and outside your head, and simply observe the pain without emotion.

Press your thumbs on the back of your neck where it joins the base of the skull, with one thumb on each side. Apply firm but comfortable pressure for a minute or more, while you breathe slowly and deeply. Each time you inhale, imagine taking clear light blue air into your lungs. See the soothing blue air rise into your head and gently swirl around inside your skull.

After a minute or so, let go of your neck and press one index finger to your "third eye" (located between the eyebrows where the nose and forehead join). Continue breathing in blue air for a minute or two. Release the pressure on your third eye and hold your index fingers to your temples. Apply pressure for at least a minute, while you inhale healing blue light, then release. Open your eyes. Repeat as necessary.

SPELL TO EASE A HEADACHE

Here's another spell to soothe a headache—especially one caused by tension or sleeplessness. Performing this relaxing ritual every day may also have a beneficial effect on blood pressure, anxiety, insomnia, digestive complaints, and other stress-related conditions.

INGREDIENTS/TOOLS:
- 1 smoky quartz crystal
- 1 piece of rose quartz
- Lavender-scented incense
- Incense burner
- Matches or a lighter

BEST TIME TO PERFORM THE SPELL:
- As needed

Wash the stones in running water, then charge them by letting them sit in the sunlight for several minutes. Place the incense in the burner and light it. Sit quietly in a comfortable spot and begin breathing slowly and deeply. Hold the rose quartz in your left hand and feel it gently emitting loving, peaceful vibrations. Hold the smoky quartz crystal to your forehead and imagine the quartz dispersing the pain. Spend as much time as you need in this calm, relaxed state. When you're finished, cleanse the stones again and set them in a sunny spot.

SPELL TO RELIEVE MOTION SICKNESS

Whether you're sailing, flying, or winding around the mountains in an RV, motion sickness can turn your dream trip into a nightmare. Motion sickness usually occurs when you feel you are out of control—notice that the driver of a car rarely gets sick. This spell helps balance your equilibrium and calm nausea.

INGREDIENTS/TOOLS:
- Sea-Bands (available online, and at some health food stores or pharmacies in packages of two)
- 1 small vial of peppermint essential oil
- Gemstone Necklace for a Safe Trip (see Chapter 11)

BEST TIME TO PERFORM THE SPELL:
- As needed

If you start to feel queasy—or worry that you might—slip the Sea-Bands onto your wrists. They should fit snugly, with the nub pressing firmly against the middle of the underside of your arm about two or three finger widths up from the bend at your wrist. Inhale a few whiffs of the peppermint essential oil—you can pour a little oil on a handkerchief or sniff it directly from the bottle.

Don your Gemstone Necklace for a Safe Trip. Feel its magick protecting you, keeping you safe despite rough seas, air turbulence, or treacherous roads. Envision yourself surrounded by a ball of pure white light that shields you from harm. If you wish, visualize guardian angels or other deities on all sides, guiding you to safety. Repeat the affirmation "I am safe and sound at all times and in all situations" until you stop feeling upset.

HEALING MILK BATH

Nearly 3,000 years ago, Hippocrates, the "father of medicine," recommended baths for all sorts of ailments, and for centuries people have "taken the waters" to remedy health problems of all kinds. This simple milk bath soothes body and mind—adapt it to your special needs by adding appropriate herbs or flowers, essential oils, bath salts, and other ingredients.

INGREDIENTS/TOOLS:

- 1 cup cornstarch
- 2 cups milk powder
- 2 tablespoons dry herbs (see the table at the beginning of this chapter for suggestions)
- 1 glass jar with lid that will hold 3 cups (24 ounces)

BEST TIME TO PERFORM THE SPELL:

- As needed

Place all the ingredients in a blender or food processor. Blend until combined and reduced to a fine powder. Pour into the jar. To use, add ½ cup of this magick blend to bathwater while the tub is filling. (Store the rest in your fridge.) Soak in the tub as long as you like. Alternate suggestion: Substitute essential oils for dry herbs: eucalyptus for colds, sandalwood for aches/pains, etc.

MAGICK HEALING BREW

You're feeling under the weather and could use a little magick to soothe what ails you. When you drink this healing brew, you nourish your body, mind, and spirit with herbal medicine and loving energy.

INGREDIENTS/TOOLS:

- Mint herbal tea
- 1 chalice (or cup)
- 1 echinacea capsule (available in health food stores and some supermarkets)
- Lemon juice, to taste
- Honey, to taste
- 1 spoon

BEST TIME TO PERFORM THE SPELL:

- As needed

Brew the mint tea and pour some into your chalice or cup. Open the echina-cea capsule and sprinkle the herb into the tea. Add a little lemon juice and honey. Stir the tea in the chalice three times, in a clockwise direction, to charge it.

Gaze at the chalice and imagine a ray of pink light flowing into the chalice, infusing the tea with healing energy. Then slowly sip the tea. Feel its loving vibrations being absorbed into your body. Let them spread out from your stomach into your arms, legs, and head. Feel a tingling warmth radiating in your heart chakra. Allow the healing herbal blend to ease your discomfort and restore your sense of well-being. Repeat as necessary.

SWEET DREAMS SPELL

When you lie down to sleep at night, does your mind keep racing like a hamster on a treadmill? If you can't stop thinking about all the things you have to do tomorrow, try this bedtime ritual—it helps you relax and get a good night's sleep, so your mind and body can rejuvenate themselves.

INGREDIENTS/TOOLS:
- 1 piece of amethyst
- 1 dark blue votive candle
- Matches or a lighter
- White Chestnut flower essence (available from health food stores or online)
- 1 glass of spring water
- 1 piece of paper
- 1 pen or pencil

BEST TIME TO PERFORM THE SPELL:
- Before going to bed

Wash the amethyst with mild soap and water, and pat it dry. Light the votive candle and spend a few moments gazing into the flame to relax your mind. Put 4 drops of White Chestnut flower essence in the glass of water and sip it slowly. On the paper, make a list of all the things you must remember to do tomorrow. Once you've written down these tasks your mind can stop reminding you of them.

When you've finished noting everything you can think of, turn the paper over and draw the *I Ching* hexagram "T'ai/Peace" on it. This symbol consists of six lines stacked one on top of the other. Each of the top three lines looks like two dashes side by side. The bottom three lines are solid. Lay the piece of paper on your nightstand with the *I Ching* hexagram facing up. Set the amethyst on top of the symbol.

Extinguish the candle. Get into bed and feel the soothing resonances of the flower essence and the amethyst quieting your thoughts. If your mind strays to worrisome matters, gently stop yourself and replace those thoughts with a mental image of the symbol "T'ai." Additional suggestion: Do this spell at least 15 minutes after brushing your teeth, as mint toothpaste or mouthwash will nullify the effects of the White Chestnut.

SWEET DREAMS POTION

According to WebMD, lack of sleep can lead to coronary problems, stroke, diabetes, and automobile accidents. We need our sleep in order to thrive, yet a huge number of people report not getting enough quality shuteye. Here's another way to quiet your thoughts and emotions so you can sleep better. This magick potion also inspires prophetic dreams that can offer guidance in your waking hours.

INGREDIENTS/TOOLS:
- 1 bowl (preferably silver or clear glass)
- 1 moonstone
- Spring water
- 1 glass bottle with a cap or stopper, any size

BEST TIME TO PERFORM THE SPELL:
- On the night of the full moon; however, if you can't wait that long, do the spell as needed

Wash the bowl and the moonstone with mild soap and water, then place the stone in the bowl. Fill the bowl with spring water. Set it on a windowsill, countertop, table, or other surface where the moon will be reflected in the water. Allow the water to sit overnight. In the morning, remove the moonstone and pour the moon-imprinted water into the bottle.

Each night before retiring, sip a little of the potion to help you sleep better. Pay attention to your dreams, too—they may hold answers to daily dilemmas or offer glimpses into the future. Make a new batch of Sweet Dreams Potion at each full moon.

SPELL TO HEAL A MINOR WOUND

This spell uses a poppet or doll to represent the injured individual—whatever you do to the doll manifests in the person you seek to heal. Remember to obtain the permission of another person before you do the spell for him or her. (This spell is intended to assist healing, not to replace professional medical care or to treat serious injuries.)

INGREDIENTS/TOOLS:
- 1 piece of cotton or silk cloth, 12" × 12", that matches the skin color of the person who seeks healing
- Straight pins
- Markers in a variety of colors
- Scissors
- Needle and thread to match the cloth
- Filling to stuff the poppet (cotton batting, wool, straw, or other material)
- Yarn that matches the hair color of the individual (or, if possible, actual hair from the person for whom you are doing the spell)
- Paper or parchment
- Herbs and/or flowers that correspond to the nature of the wound
- Green, blue, or white cloth

BEST TIME TO PERFORM THE SPELL:
- As needed

Fold the skin-colored cloth in half and pin it together. With a marker trace a basic human shape on the top layer of the cloth. Don't make it too small; use as much space as you can on the cloth. Cut out the

The Modern Witchcraft Spell Book

human shape, cutting through both layers of cloth at the same time. You will have two flat, human-like shapes. Match the edges and pin the two shapes together. Sew them together with a small running stitch (it's better to do this by hand rather than with a sewing machine, because it's more personal and gives you more time to focus on your intention). Leave one side of the "body" open between the hip and the arm.

Stuff the poppet with whatever material you've chosen. Pin the hole shut temporarily. With the markers, personalize the poppet to look like the individual who will be healed. Add yarn for hair, or attach clippings of the person's real hair. Draw eyes, nose, mouth, and other features. Add any physical markings such as birthmarks or tattoos. Enrich the poppet's appearance with colors that correspond to the individual's own characteristics. Write the person's full name and birthdate on the slip of paper, and fold it up. Unpin the hole and tuck the folded paper inside the doll. Pin it shut again. Hold the doll in your hands and look it into its eyes. State aloud the person's name with confidence and awareness. Visualize him or her whole and well—don't focus on the injury.

Unpin the hole, and gather up pinches of the herbs you have selected to correspond with healing the wound. Tuck them into the doll. Sew the hole up, as you say:

"Needle and thread,
Knit bone to bone,
Flesh to flesh,
Cell to cell.
[Name], you are well."

Hold the poppet in your hands and hum a single note. (You may choose to hum a note that corresponds to the chakra linked with the injury; see Chapter 2.) As you hum, visualize healing energy flowing down your arms and into the doll. When you feel as if the doll holds as much energy as it can handle for the moment, wrap it gently in the cloth whose color you've chosen to represent healing. Place the poppet in a safe place.

You may repeat the healing hum once a day if the individual requires it. When the person has recovered and is well again, thank the doll for its help. Then hold it in your hands and look it in the eyes. State aloud, with confidence and awareness: "This is no longer [name]." Burn or bury the doll to symbolize that the healing is complete and the poppet has served its purpose. Alternate suggestion: If the individual is chronically ill, do not destroy the doll, but keep it as a focus for ongoing healing work. You may ask the person if he or she would like you to keep the poppet in order to strengthen the healing process.

EASY DOES IT LOTION

You've overdone it and now your muscles are making their displeasure known. This herbal balm helps soothe sore muscles and relieve minor aches and pains.

INGREDIENTS/TOOLS:
- 1 glass jar, bottle, or other container with a lid
- 1 small clear quartz crystal
- 4 ounces of olive, grape seed, or almond oil
- A few drops of camphor essential oil
- A few drops of clove essential oil
- A few drops of lavender essential oil
- 1 small amount of fresh ginger root, grated very fine

BEST TIME TO PERFORM THE SPELL:
- As needed

Wash the jar or bottle and the crystal with mild soap and water. Pour the olive, grape seed, or almond oil into the bottle. Add a few drops of each essential oil. Add the fresh ginger to the oil mixture. Hold the quartz crystal to your "third eye" (between your eyebrows) and send a vision of soothing, healing energy into the crystal. You might see it as blue or green light. Then put the crystal into the oil mixture and cap the jar/bottle. Shake the jar/bottle three times to charge it. Rub the healing lotion on your sore muscles to alleviate pain. Repeat as necessary.

HEAVEN AND EARTH RITUAL TO INCREASE VITALITY

This ritual invites the nurturing, supportive energy of the earth and the enlivening energy of the sun to blend within your body and bring balance. If possible, perform this ritual outside, in a safe place where you can burn candles.

INGREDIENTS/TOOLS:
- 4 bayberry candles in holders (votive candles in glass containers are good choices)
- Matches or a lighter
- 4 clear quartz crystals

BEST TIME TO PERFORM THIS SPELL:
- As needed

Place the candles at the four compass directions. Set the crystals between the candles to form a circle. You'll notice this eight-point circle resembles the Wheel of the Year (discussed in Chapter 8). Step inside the circle and light the candles, beginning in the east and working in a clockwise direction. Stand facing east, with your arms outstretched at your sides, parallel to the ground, palms up.

The candles represent the fire element and the masculine force. The crystals symbolize the earth element and the feminine force. Feel the balanced energy around you flowing into your body from every direction. Receive it in your open hands and allow it to fill you up, energizing you. Draw Mother Earth's nurturing energy upward through your feet, into your legs, torso, arms, and head. Feel the sun's vitalizing energy flowing into the top of your head and down through your body, all the way to your feet. Envision the two forces—yin and yang, heaven and earth—blending and balancing one another in your heart center.

Stand in the center of the circle as long as you choose. When you feel invigorated, extinguish the candles in a counterclockwise direction to open the circle, and pick up the crystals. Carry the crystals with you to continually charge yourself with positive energy, or place them at the corners of your home to provide extra energy. Repeat this spell as often as needed. If you wish, you can invite other people to join you in the healing circle.

KEEP YOUR COOL POTION

This magick potion helps you beat the heat, whether it's physical or psychological. The secret ingredient is aquamarine, a pale blue gem whose name comes from the Latin word for seawater. Wise men and women used this stone to calm anger, ease stress, lower blood pressure, and bring down fevers.

INGREDIENTS/TOOLS:
- 1 aquamarine
- 1 chalice (or clear glass)
- Spring water

BEST TIME TO PERFORM THE SPELL:
- Anytime

Wash the aquamarine and chalice/glass with mild soap and water to remove any ambient vibrations and/or dirt. Place the gem in the bottom of your chalice, then fill the chalice with water. Swirl the water in the chalice in a counterclockwise direction to charge it, while you chant the following incantation:

"I am healed
In body and mind
Of imbalances
Of any kind."

Remove the aquamarine. As you drink the potion, imagine you are immersing yourself in a refreshing pool of water to help you keep your cool. Store unused water in the fridge, preferably in a clear glass bottle, and keep some on hand for emergencies. Additional suggestion: You can also soak a clean cotton cloth in this magick potion to make a cooling poultice. Lay the cloth on your forehead to ease a headache, over your eyes to soothe eyestrain, or on your abdomen to aid hot flashes or menstrual cramps.

RITUAL TO RECLAIM YOUR ENERGY

Do you feel worn out at the end of the day, especially if you have to deal with a lot of people? When you're around a difficult person, do you notice your energy diminishing? According to ancient Toltec teachings, you leave a bit of your own vitality behind with every individual you meet during the day. This ritual lets you reclaim the energy you've given away, so you don't get depleted.

INGREDIENTS/TOOLS:
• None

BEST TIME TO PERFORM THE SPELL:
• At the end of each day, before going to sleep

Sit in a comfortable chair and close your eyes. Start breathing slowly and deeply. Begin recalling all the people you encountered and all the incidents that occurred during the day, one at a time.

Turn your head to the left and remember something that happened in which you participated in some way. Inhale as you revisit the thoughts and feelings you had, as well as the actions that took place. Then turn your head to the right and exhale, releasing the experience with your breath. Continue doing this until you've recapped every event of the day, from beginning to end, the little things as well as the big ones. Feel yourself relaxing and gaining strength with each memory you cast out.

HEALING CHICKEN AND VEGGIE SOUP

Soup is a delicious way to warm up in the winter—especially if you're suffering with a cold or flu. In this recipe, the chicken and vegetables support the immune system to fight illness. The magickal secret to this soup's healing power comes not only from the vitamins and minerals in the ingredients, but also from the positive, loving vibrations you focus into the brew while you're cooking it.

INGREDIENTS/TOOLS:
• 4 tablespoons butter

- Large saucepan
- 1 large white onion, chopped
- 3 cloves garlic, diced
- 3 tablespoons brown sugar
- 2 tablespoons flour
- 4 cups chicken stock
- 1 (14½-ounce) can of diced tomatoes with juice
- 2 large carrots
- 2 large potatoes
- 1 small bunch of kale, chopped
- 2 tablespoons fresh parsley, chopped
- Water, as needed
- Salt and freshly ground pepper, to taste
- ¼ cup sherry or port (optional)
- Baguette (French bread), or croutons
- 1 cup grated mozzarella cheese

1. Melt the butter in the saucepan. Add the onion, garlic, and sugar and cook over medium-high heat; stir constantly using a clockwise motion (to boost the soup's healing energy) for 15 minutes or until sticky and caramel-brown. Remove from the heat.
2. Stir in the flour. Slowly add the stock, again stirring constantly using a clockwise motion. Return to the heat and bring to a boil, stirring regularly.
3. Add the veggies—feel free to include or substitute other vegetables if you wish (see tables in Chapter 16 for magickal correspondences). If soup seems too thick, add water (or more chicken stock or vegetable juice) until you get the consistency you like. Add salt and pepper to taste.
4. Cover and simmer gently for a half-hour (or longer if you wish), stirring occasionally. Add the sherry or port (if using). Taste and adjust the seasoning if required. Serve hot in bowls. Garnish with a slice of toasted baguette or croutons; sprinkle with grated cheese and chopped parsley.

Chapter 14

SPELLS FOR SELF-IMPROVEMENT

Self-doubt and lack of self-worth are common problems for many people. Self-esteem issues can keep you from achieving success in your career, from becoming financially secure, or from finding the love you desire and deserve. They can even cause illness. Increasing your sense of your own worthiness will help you to enhance every area of your life. You'll also improve your magickal power so you can produce better, faster results.

> *"Think of yourself like this: There's a universal intelligence subsisting throughout nature inherent in every one of its manifestations. You are one of those manifestations. You are a piece of this universal intelligence—a slice of God, if you will."*
> —DR. WAYNE W. DYER, *THE POWER OF INTENTION*

Regardless of what area in your life you wish to improve—your appearance, your health, your musical or athletic ability, your intelligence or intuition—magick can help. The most important part of working magick is your intent, fueled by your desire and willpower. Spells may not build up your physical muscles—although they can increase your energy and determination to stick with your training program—but they work wonders for strengthening your mental "muscles." The very nature of spellcasting requires you to focus your mind and use your imagination to visualize outcomes.

The spells in this chapter cover a wide range of conditions and objectives, from strengthening your sense of security to clearing your skin to eliminating an old habit. The tables included here offer information about the ingredients to use in spellwork, according to your purposes. Feel free to substitute ingredients from these charts to customize your spells and make them more personal.

Steps for Successful Spellcasting

Whenever you cast a spell, remember to use a few tried-and-true measures, as described in Chapter 1. These precautions can help you avoid complications, mix-ups, delays, or disappointments:

1. Remove all distractions.
2. Collect the ingredients and tools you'll use in your spell and cleanse them.
3. Purify and sanctify your space.
4. Quiet your mind.
5. Cast a circle around the area where you'll do your spellworking.
6. Perform the spell.
7. If you've called upon deities or spirits to assist you, thank and release them.
8. Open the circle.
9. Store your tools in a safe place until you need them again.

The Modern Witchcraft Spell Book

COLORS TO USE IN SPELLS FOR PERSONAL IMPROVEMENT

To enhance the spells you do for personal improvement, incorporate the colors yellow or orange into your workings. If your intention includes healing of some sort, you might also use green and/or blue. If you feel a need for more self-love and acceptance, choose pink. The most popular ways to bring in these colors are to burn candles or craft talisman pouches in these colors. You may also want to carry gemstones in these colors as talismans, or wear these colors while performing spells. Add flower petals that remind you of your objectives to mojo bags, ritual baths, sachets, or potions. Many of the spells in this chapter use these color associations.

INGREDIENTS FOR PERSONAL IMPROVEMENT SPELLS
Gemstones
Aquamarine: Stimulates intuition, imagination, and creativity
Fluorite: Improves concentration and mental clarity
Lapis lazuli: Deepens insight and inner wisdom
Moldavite: Enhances your ability to communicate with spirits, deities, and extraterrestrials
Obsidian: Provides strength to face obstacles; helps you break old habits
Sapphire: Increases spiritual knowledge and connection with the Divine
Flowers
Carnation: Promotes strength and perseverance
Rose: Pink increases self-love and yellow enhances creativity
Sunflower: Boosts confidence
Essential Oils/Incense
Anise: Improves psychic vision
Bergamot: Elevates your mood and increases confidence
Lemon: Clears the mind and makes you more alert
Orange: Increases happiness and optimism
Herbs and Spices
Marjoram: Encourages cooperation; supports life changes
Sage: Improves memory; clears old attitudes
Thyme: Strengthens focus and concentration
Verbena: Increases skill in artistic areas, especially performance

SPELL TO STRENGTHEN THE FIRST CHAKRA

This spell focuses on the body's first major energy center, known as the root chakra, at the base of your spine, to strengthen your sense of security, stability, and inner power.

Ingredients/Tools:
- 1 object that represents your "tribe"
- 1 pen
- 1 piece of paper
- 1 red candle in a holder
- Vial of clove essential oil
- Matches or a lighter

Best time to perform the spell:
- During the waxing moon, preferably when the sun or moon is in Aries or Leo

The tribe symbol should be an object that represents your support system—a family photo, a figurine of a totem animal, or a treasured heirloom or item from your past. Set this "power object" on your altar. Next, write an affirmation that describes your intention. For example, you might write: "I can handle any challenge that comes my way" or "I am capable of caring for myself and my loved ones." Fold the paper three times and slip it under the object that signifies your tribe.

Dress the candle with clove oil (not on the wick). If you wish, dab some oil on your power object, too, and at the base of your spine. As you light the candle, inhale the scent of clove and say your affirmation aloud. Focus on the spot at the base of your spine and imagine you are directing energy into it. Imagine a glowing ball of red light there. Allow the candle to burn down on its own, and then burn the paper, releasing your affirmation into the universe.

COLOR SPELL FOR REVISING YOUR LIFE

This spell helps improve your life—even if you can't put your finger on precisely what or how it might make things better. The key is remembering that you are in charge of your own life—not somebody else—and every moment you have the power to change the things you don't like about it.

INGREDIENTS/TOOLS:
- 1 piece of white paper
- 1 box of crayons (with at least 7 colors in the box)

BEST TIME TO PERFORM THE SPELL:
- During the new moon, preferably when the sun or moon is in Aries, or on a Tuesday, Thursday, or Sunday

Draw a big circle on the paper. This circle represents your life. Divide the circle into pie-slice wedges, as many wedges as you feel are necessary. Designate each slice to represent a segment of your life: friends, money, family, health, career, love—whatever you deem important. Usually we associate certain colors with certain areas of our lives: pink with love and affection, gold with money, etc. (At the beginning of the chapters in Part II of this book, you'll find information about colors to use in various types of spells and their meanings—but if your personal associations are different, by all means go with them.)

Look at the wedges that you've identified in your circle. Which areas of your life are you happy with and which ones do you want to change? Then look at the colors in your box of crayons and consider how those colors relate to your objectives. For example, if you want to relieve job-related stress and you connect serenity with blue, color the job sector blue. If you seek more affection in your love life, color that wedge pink. If you aren't clear about what you want to change, choose the crayon(s) you feel most drawn to at this moment and let your intuition guide you.

As you color the wedges in your circle, visualize your life realigning and rebalancing to reflect your choices. Don't be concerned about staying in the lines. Life isn't neatly compartmentalized. It's messy. Recognize that, accept it, and embrace it. You can also decorate your circular chart with stickers, glitter, cut-out photos, words, or whatever you like to personalize it. It's your life—have fun! Display your finished drawing on your altar, your desk, the fridge, the bathroom mirror, or another place where you'll see it often. Each time you look at it, reaffirm your commitment to creating the ideal balance of energies in your life.

CLEAR SKIN RITUAL

Do you see pimples, wrinkles, or other "imperfections" when you look into your mirror? When you do this simple ritual you focus positive energy onto your face to clear and rejuvenate your skin.

INGREDIENTS/TOOLS:
• None

BEST TIME TO PERFORM THE SPELL:
• Every day

Close your eyes and begin breathing slowly and deeply. Rub your palms together vigorously, until they feel quite warm. Beginning at your collarbones, hold your hands an inch or so away from your body with your palms turned toward you. Move your hands upward, over your face, to the top of your head—but don't actually touch your face. When you get to the top of your head, flick your hands sharply as if throwing off water—you are actually shaking off unwanted energy.

As you move your hands, imagine you are drawing off all the tension and impurities that lead to wrinkles, pimples, dryness, discoloration, and other imperfections. Envision healing, invigorating energy infusing your skin with good energy. Repeat these movements six more times (for a total of seven passes). Perform this quick-and-easy ritual each morning and each night to stimulate your own inherent vitality and regenerative abilities.

USE AN ANIMAL TOKEN TO ENHANCE A QUALITY

If you'd like to enhance a particular quality in yourself, look at the animal kingdom to see which creature embodies the quality you seek. The owl, for example, symbolizes wisdom; the lion represents courage; the turtle displays determination.

Ingredients/Tools:

- 1 candle of a color that corresponds to your intention or that reminds you of the animal you've chosen
- 1 candleholder
- Matches or a lighter
- 1 small square of aluminum foil, 4" × 4"
- 1 nail, dry ballpoint pen, or other sharp object

Best time to perform this spell:

- On the new moon

Fit the candle in the candleholder and light it. Allow it to burn while you meditate upon the animal you have chosen. Consider the qualities you admire in this creature and how you will use those characteristics in your own life. Carefully pick up the candle and hold it horizontally. Allow the wax to drip onto the piece of aluminum foil, forming a circular shape about the size of a quarter. Make sure the wax is at least ⅛" thick, and try to keep it as even as possible. Allow the wax to cool and dry. Leave the candle to burn while you work.

Peel the wax off the aluminum foil and turn it over so that the smooth side is facing up. With the nail, pen, or other tool, lightly scratch a simple symbol into the wax that represents the animal you have chosen. Do not carve too deeply, or you will snap the wax disk. Hold the wax amulet in your hands and envision the animal you have chosen, as you say:

"O [animal], lend me your [quality]
[Quality] flow through me night and day, day and night.
These are my words, this is my will.
So mote it be."

If you like, you can even act like the animal to show that you are receiving the animal energy you desire. Roar like the lion, hoot like the owl, etc. Hold the wax circle to your heart as you visualize the quality you seek flowing into you, down your arms, and into the wax circle. Extinguish the candle. Carry the wax disk with you to continue bringing you wisdom, courage, or whatever quality you seek.

BANISH THE BLUES

If you've been singing the blues lately, this ritual helps you change your tune. Drumming stimulates acupressure and reflexology points on your hands to produce beneficial effects. Because the beats harmonize with the beating of your own heart, drumming makes you feel joyful and alive.

INGREDIENTS/TOOLS:
- Sandalwood incense
- Incense burner
- Matches or a lighter
- Brightly colored ribbons (number and colors optional)
- 1 hand drum (for instance, a djembe, doumbek, or conga)
- The Sun card from a tarot deck you don't use for readings

BEST TIME TO PERFORM THE SPELL:
- Anytime

Fit the incense in its holder and light it. Tie the ribbons on the drum, as many as you like, in whatever colors please you. Then attach the Sun card to the drum, with the image facing out (you may be able to simply slip it under the drum strings).

Begin playing the drum with both hands. Don't worry about how you sound or whether you're doing it right, just play. Feel the drum's vibrations resonating through your hands, arms, and body. Feel it breaking up the dense, depressing energy around you. Close your eyes if you like. Try a variety of beats, keeping your mind focused on your drumming. You may hear singing or sense the presence of nonphysical beings near you, for drumming attracts fun-loving spirits. If you wish, put on a CD of lively African or Caribbean music and play along with it. Continue playing as long as you like. Repeat this spell whenever you start feeling blue to quickly shift your emotions to a higher vibration.

A LIGHT IN THE DARKNESS

If you don't feel you're getting the attention or respect you deserve, perhaps it's because other people can't see the real you. This spell makes them sit up and take notice, as you shine your light into the darkness like a beacon.

INGREDIENTS/TOOLS:
- 1 tarot card that represents you (from a deck you don't normally use for readings)
- 7 purple candles in candleholders
- Matches or a lighter

BEST TIME TO PERFORM THE SPELL:
- Begin 7 days before the full moon

Choose a tarot card that you resonate with or that you feel depicts you. Lay the card face up on your altar or another spot where you can leave the spell components safely in place for a week. Arrange the candles in a tight circle around the card. Light the candles, starting with the candle at the top of the card and working your way around the circle in a clockwise direction until you've lit them all. Gaze at the setup for a few moments while you imagine yourself illuminated brilliantly, as if standing in a spotlight. See other people watching and admiring you. When you feel ready, extinguish the candles in a counterclockwise direction.

The next day, repeat the ritual. This time, however, widen the circle of candles by moving each candle outward an inch or two. Repeat the ritual for a total of 7 days, moving the candles apart a little more each day. As the circle of candles increases in size, you expand your personal power. The light you shine into the world burns brighter and touches more people. On the night of the full moon allow the candles to finish burning down completely to send your "light" out into the universe. (Remember not to leave lit candles unattended.)

SPELL TO RELEASE OUTMODED PATTERNS

Identify one or more patterns that are holding you back or limiting your ability to express yourself. Choose candles of a color that relates to your objective. If you want to be better at handling your financial investments, for instance, use gold or silver candles. If you want to be more creative in your professional life, use orange candles. If you want to be kinder and more loving toward yourself and others, burn pink candles.

INGREDIENTS/TOOLS:
- 2 candles in a color that corresponds to your intentions
- 1 piece of string
- Matches or a lighter
- Scissors
- Cauldron (optional)

BEST TIME TO PERFORM THE SPELL:
- During the waning moon, on a Saturday, or when the sun or moon is in Capricorn

Set the candles on your altar and tie them together with the string. Light the candles. Imagine the string is a limiting force that binds you and keeps you from functioning as fully as you could. Feel the energy of that self-limiting bond. Let your emotions come to the surface until they reach a peak and you experience a strong desire to remove the fetters. Then cut the string and burn it in your cauldron. (If you don't have a cauldron, you can burn it in the fireplace, a barbecue grill, or other safe place.) Say aloud:

"My self-limiting beliefs and bonds
Are burned up in this cleansing fire.
I'm now free to express myself
In any way I choose and desire."

Sense the relief that accompanies this symbolic release. Know that you can do whatever you wish to do, now that you've removed the old restrictions.

ANGELIC SPELL FOR CREATIVE ENERGY

If you feel a special affinity with a certain angel or deity, invite him or her to participate in this spell with you. Or ask one of the deities associated with creativity—Brigid, Isis, Apollo, Lugh, Odin, or Thoth, for example—to assist you.

INGREDIENTS/TOOLS:
- 1 small statue, icon, charm, picture, or other likeness of the angel or deity
- An offering for the angel or deity (your choice)

BEST TIME TO PERFORM THE SPELL
- During the waxing moon, especially when the sun or moon is in Leo or Libra; at dawn on a Sunday or Friday

Stand in the center of your circle and hold the likeness of the angel or deity in your hands. Invite him or her to fill you with creative power and join you in whatever task you've chosen. Then call upon the spirits of the four elements to lend their energies, too. Say aloud:

"Spirits of Air, fill me with inspiration.
Spirits of Fire, fill me with passion.
Spirits of Water, fill me with imagination.
Spirits of Earth, fill me with patience."

Feel the energies of these spirits—under the direction of your angel or deity—flowing into you. Stand in the circle as long as you like. When you feel you've absorbed as much creative energy as you need, place the image of the angel or deity on your altar. Lay the offering (a flower, a gemstone, or whatever you've selected) in front of the image and express your thanks. Release the entities you've called upon, with gratitude. Whenever you feel a need for a creative boost, touch the image and know that your guardian will assist you.

FENG SHUI SPELL TO ENHANCE CREATIVITY

Maybe you don't think of yourself as being creative, but everyone has some creative talent. Often we stifle ourselves because we think we have to be a Mozart or van Gogh. This spell uses the Chinese magickal art of feng shui to spark your imagination and get your creative juices flowing.

INGREDIENTS/TOOLS:
- 1 slip of paper
- 1 pen
- 3 coins (any denomination)
- 1 bowl
- Yellow rose petals

BEST TIME TO PERFORM THE SPELL:
- When the moon is waxing, preferably when the sun or moon is in Leo

To locate the area of your home that corresponds to creativity, stand at the doorway that you use most often to enter or exit your home, facing in. Halfway between the farthest right-hand corner and the nearest right-hand corner is the creativity sector.

Write an affirmation on a slip of paper, describing your intention. Remember to state it in the present tense. For example, you might write "A major publishing company now buys my novel and I am content with all aspects of the contract." Or you could state "I now land a role in the upcoming community play" or "My tulips win an award in the spring gardening show."

Place your written affirmation in the creativity sector of your home, then position the three coins on top of it. The coins symbolize receiving money (or other rewards) for your creativity. Next, set the bowl on top of the coins and the affirmation. The bowl represents your willingness to attract and hold on to creative ideas. Fill the bowl with the rose petals. Yellow, the color associated with creativity and self-esteem, suggests that your creative ideas are blossoming and taking shape in the material world. Leave this spell in place until the full moon or until your wish materializes.

FENG SHUI SPELL TO IMPROVE YOUR IMAGE

Have you ever noticed that the entrances to the homes of rich and pow-erful people—as well as doors leading into government buildings, suc-cessful businesses, and cathedrals—tend to be grand, easily accessible, and well lit? In feng shui, the entrance to your home corresponds to your self-image and identity. Observe your entryway. Is it attractive and inviting? Or is it nondescript, cluttered, dark, maybe even difficult to find? To change your image—and the impression you make on others—all you have to do is improve your home's entrance.

INGREDIENTS/TOOLS:
• Whatever you choose

BEST TIME TO PERFORM THE SPELL:
• During the waxing moon, preferably when the sun or moon is in Leo, or on the summer solstice

Here are some ways you can improve your image: Install better light-ing. Put a large, attractive plant near the door. Paint the door a bright, cheerful color. Affix handsome brass numerals on the door. Hang a deco-rative wreath on the door. Clear away all clutter or obstacles. Fix broken steps and railings. Remember, this is the first impression your visitors get of you, so make it as appealing as possible.

While you're working, periodically repeat this incantation (or anoth-er that you've designed yourself):

"The updates that I make today
Enhance my image in every way."

Keep your intention in mind—that's the most important part of the spell.

TALISMAN TO INCREASE SELF-CONFIDENCE

Most of us tend to be a little too self-critical. We pay more attention to our shortcomings than to our strengths and talents. This spell combines a selection of ingredients that encourage personal power and fire up self-confidence.

Ingredients/Tools:

- 1 piece of paper
- 1 pen, marker, or colored pencil
- 1 gold-colored pouch, preferably made of silk
- 1 almond
- 1 pinch of sage
- 1 acorn
- 1 small piece of tiger's eye, carnelian, or red jasper
- 1 red ribbon
- Sandalwood incense in a holder
- Matches or a lighter

Best time to perform the spell:

- On the full moon, preferably a Sunday or a Thursday, or when the sun or moon is in Leo

As described in Chapter 5, design a magick sigil by entwining the letters that spell the word *power* so they form an image. Fold the paper three times, then slip it into the gold-colored pouch. Add the almond, sage, acorn, and stone. Tie the pouch with the red ribbon, making 9 knots. Each time you tie a knot, repeat this incantation:

"By the magick of three times three
Divine power flows through me.
I am all I wish to be."

Light the incense. Hold the talisman in the smoke for a few moments to charge it. Carry the talisman with you to increase your self-confidence. Hold it in your hand whenever you feel a need for a confidence boost. If you prefer, put it on your altar or in a spot where you'll see it often.

QUICK AND EASY SPELL FOR EMPOWERMENT

This spell requires no tools except the belief that magick works and that it can work for you. As you're waking up in the morning, before you open your eyes, when you're still in that drowsy state halfway between dreams and full consciousness, visualize whatever it is that you desire. The first thoughts you have in the morning are very powerful, and they color your experiences throughout the day. Then say your wish silently to yourself, in the form of an affirmation.

Let's say you want to ace an exam. Visualize the end result as vividly as possible: a big red A at the top of your exam sheet. Pour emotion into it. Imagine how excited you'll be when you see the A. Then say to yourself, "I ace my exam," feeling confident that you will do just that. When you get out of bed, forget about it. Release the desire and don't worry. Assuming that you've done your part to get an A on the exam (studied or otherwise prepared yourself), your intention should come true.

TAKE BACK WHAT'S YOURS

If you've let other people drain your energy during the day, this ritual will help you take back what's yours. Do this colorful practice every evening to improve your vitality, strengthen your ability to accomplish your objectives, and enhance every area of your life.

INGREDIENTS/TOOLS:
- None

BEST TIME TO PERFORM THE SPELL:
- At the end of each day, before going to sleep

Sit in a comfortable chair and close your eyes. Start breathing slowly and deeply. Bring to mind someone you encountered during the day. Imagine that person standing in front of you. Notice any splotches of color that appear to be stuck onto that person's body—they represent pieces of your own vital energy that you gave away to someone else.

Pick one splotch and as you inhale, imagine you are pulling that colored energy patch off the person's body and drawing it toward yourself.

As you exhale, feel the energy being reabsorbed into your body. Notice how this makes you feel—you should experience a slight sensation of contentment and strength.

Continue in this manner until you've taken back all the energy you lost during the day. You'll know you're done when you don't see any more colored blotches remaining on that individual's body. Then call to mind another person and repeat the ritual. Do this for everyone with whom you interacted, so they don't keep draining your power.

TRUE COLORS

Have daily stress and worries thrown you off-balance? This magick visualization technique tones your chakras to restore harmony to your entire system. When your chakras are balanced, you feel better in body, mind, and spirit.

Ingredients/Tools:
- None

Best time to perform the spell:
- Anytime

Sit in a comfortable chair and close your eyes. Start breathing slowly and deeply. Focus your attention on the base of your spine, the energy center known as the "root chakra." Imagine a ball of clear red light glowing there, and feel warmth radiating in this part of your body for a few moments. Next, focus on the "sacral chakra" about a hand's width below your belly button. Envision a sphere of orange light shining there. After a few moments shift your attention to your solar plexus; see yellow light radiating there and warming this part of your body.

Continue breathing rhythmically as you visualize bright green light glowing around your heart. Feel it calming your emotions. Move your attention up to the base of your throat and imagine blue light shining there for a few moments. This helps you speak up for yourself with confidence. Shift your focus to your "third eye" on your forehead between your eyebrows, while you envision indigo light at this point. Finally, allow your attention to go to the "crown chakra" at the top of your head. As you see purple light glowing there, sense your connection with a higher force. Feel power flowing from the heavens into the top of your head and down your spine, energizing your entire body.

Enjoy this pleasant, soothing sensation for as long as you wish. Repeat this revitalizing ritual whenever you feel off-center, stressed out, or tired.

SPELL TO RELEASE SADNESS

This spell helps to lift your spirits by bringing back carefree feelings from childhood. On a practical level, it gets you outside in the sunshine and fresh air, and gives you a little exercise—all of which can improve your mood.

INGREDIENTS/TOOLS:
- 1 kite
- Kite string
- Strips of paper or lightweight ribbon
- Tape
- Scissors
- Matches or a lighter
- 1 cauldron (optional)

BEST TIME TO PERFORM THE SPELL:
- At sunset

Attach the string to the kite, then affix the strips of paper or ribbon to the kite's tail. Each strip or ribbon represents something that is causing you sadness. Take the kite to an open area. Feel the wind flow around you. Feel the sorrow in your heart, and imagine it flowing down your arms into the kite. Allow the wind to catch the kite and lift it up into the air. If you've never flown a kite before, abandon yourself to the experience. It takes focus, and intuition, and patience—just as magick does. As you fly the kite, visualize the wind lifting your sorrow gently away.

Fly the kite for as long as you choose. When you are done, reel it in and cut off the paper strips or ribbons. Burn them in your cauldron (or a safe spot such as a fireplace or barbecue grill) to symbolically eliminate your sadness. Repeat as often as necessary.

SPELL TO RELEASE ANGER

In order to release something, you must first acknowledge it. Holding on to anger not only drains your personal power, it also prevents good things from coming to you. This spell helps you release anger that may be eating away at you and draining energy that you could use more productively.

INGREDIENTS/TOOLS:
- 1 piece of paper
- 1 pen
- Matches or a lighter
- 1 cauldron (optional)

BEST TIME TO PERFORM THE SPELL:
- During the waning moon, at sunset on a Saturday

Write a letter to the person with whom you are angry. Use profanity, excessive exclamation points, capital letters, and bad grammar if you wish. Tell that person exactly what you think of him or her and how you feel. When you are done, reread your letter. Allow yourself to feel as emotional as you like.

Then, take three deep breaths and exhale all your tension and stress. At the bottom of your letter, write "I release my anger. [Name], you no longer hold any power over me." Burn the letter in your cauldron (or a safe spot such as a fireplace or barbecue grill) to symbolically eliminate your anger. Envision your anger drifting away with the smoke. Repeat as often as necessary, whenever a person or situation arouses your anger.

Chapter 15
SPELLS TO DO WITH OTHERS

At some point in your magickal journey you may decide to try spell-working with other people—especially if you're the sociable type and enjoy the camaraderie of like-minded folks. You've probably heard of witches' covens, but lots of magickal brotherhoods and sisterhoods have existed in the past and still do today. The Freemasons, the Hermetic Order of the Golden Dawn, and the Ordo Templi Orientis are just a few of the famous ones.

Joining forces with other magicians can strengthen your power by combining your energies and directing them toward a common purpose. Quite likely, some people in the group will have certain talents and skills, whereas others have different abilities—and that can benefit everyone. The key is to connect with people you respect and trust and whose objectives and beliefs are in harmony with your own. Problems can arise when members of the group disagree about how things should be done or power struggles get in the way of the common good. It's like what sometimes happens in businesses or social organizations—except when you're working magick, things can really get out of hand.

The spells in this chapter are designed for two or more people to perform together. Some spells also invite deities, elementals, spirit animals, and other entities to participate with you.

Steps for Successful Spellcasting

Whenever you cast a spell, remember to use a few tried-and-true measures, as described in Chapter 1. These precautions can help you avoid complications, mix-ups, delays, or disappointments:

1. Remove all distractions.
2. Collect the ingredients and tools you'll use in your spell and cleanse them.
3. Purify and sanctify your space.
4. Quiet your mind.
5. Cast a circle around the area where you'll do your spellworking.
6. Perform the spell.
7. If you've called upon deities or spirits to assist you, thank and release them.
8. Open the circle.
9. Store your tools in a safe place until you need them again.

SPELL TO CONNECT WITH OTHER MAGICIANS

If you think you'd like to do magick with other people, but don't know where to find those people, do a spell to attract them. Be as specific as you choose when you design this spell. If you wish to work only with men or women, be sure to say so. If you are open to working with an online spellcasting group, leave out the geographical conditions. If you wish to work with people of a specific religious path, then indicate that. Be aware, however, that the more conditions you stipulate, the fewer people will fill them. You have every right to be picky about the people you draw to yourself—and of course, you don't have to work with everyone you meet who happens to be a magician. This spell increases your chances of meeting people who are open to working with other spell-casters, not to lock you into a partnership of any kind.

Ingredients/Tools:
- 1 peach-colored candle
- A few drops of vanilla essential oil (or pure vanilla extract)
- Matches or a lighter
- 1 slip of paper
- 1 pen
- 1 cauldron (or heatproof bowl)
- Several little feathers

Best time to perform the spell:
- At dawn during the moon's first quarter, preferably when the sun or moon is in Aquarius

Anoint the candle with vanilla. Light it, visualizing the light expanding and serving as a beacon to guide fellow magicians to you. On the paper, write an invitation to your ideal future spellcasting partners. For example, you might write: "I, [your name], issue an invitation to honest, sincere, and true spellcasters of [your geographical area]. If you seek to meet new people with whom to work, let us find one another." Sign it. Read the invitation aloud. Visualize your words flowing out into the world.

Touch the edge of the invitation to the candle's flame. When the paper has caught fire, let it burn in the heatproof bowl or cauldron. As it burns, visualize the energy of your invitation being released to flow out into the world. Allow the bowl or cauldron to cool. Place the feathers into the cauldron. Take the cauldron outside and hold it so that the wind lifts and swirls the feathers and the ashes, carrying them out into the world. If necessary, scoop the feathers and ashes out with your hand and toss them into the air. Watch the wind whisk away the ashes and feathers, and know your request has been sent.

If you're operating within an established group of people who've gathered to cast a spell (sometimes referred to as a circle), then you'll have at least some sort of energy connection between you. The closer you are to one another, the easier it is to merge and balance your energies. This comes with practice, of course; blending energy doesn't happen perfectly on the first try, no matter how experienced you are. With practice, though, you'll find the right balance of personal energies to create the right mix.

CREATE A GROUP POWER BUNDLE

Consider doing this spell when you first start working with a group of other magicians to connect your powers. It also strengthens your sense of unity and responsibility as a circle, and can give you insight into the individuals in your group.

INGREDIENTS/TOOLS:
- Small objects of your choice
- 1 multicolored pouch that includes all 7 colors of the rainbow

BEST TIME TO PERFORM THE SPELL:
- Anytime

Ask the members of the circle to bring small objects that they feel represent them. One person might bring a small figurine of an animal, another a favorite stone or crystal, a twig from a tree, a feather—it can be anything that holds special significance for the person. If you wish, have the members explain what the objects mean to them. Place the objects in the center of your circle. Raise energy by chanting together:

"We are one, our power flows.
We are one, our power grows."

After a minute or two of chanting, you'll start to feel the energy around you growing stronger. Focus the energy with your minds and direct it into the objects. Then put the objects into the pouch to keep them safe and to contain the energy. This is your group's power bundle. If the group meets in someone's home regularly, store it there. If the location changes, assign a different person each month (or after each meeting) to take the bundle home and watch over it. Bring it out at each meeting to symbolize unity.

CHALICE SPELL TO BOND A SPELLCASTING CIRCLE

This is a great spell for making your commitment to the spellcasting group official and launching your circle. You may also want to do it periodically to reinforce your bond, for example at the eight sabbats in the Wheel of the Year.

INGREDIENTS/TOOLS:
- 1 small bottle, can, or box of fruit juice of your choice
- 1 glass pitcher
- Glasses (one for each participant)
- 1 long-handled spoon

BEST TIME TO PERFORM THE SPELL:
- During the waxing moon, preferably on a Friday or when the sun or moon is in Aquarius

Have everyone bring one kind of juice to the meeting—don't confer beforehand, let it be random. Clean the pitcher, glasses, and spoon and consecrate them for your purpose. Place the pitcher, glasses, and spoon on your altar (or a table within your circle). Ask each member to empower his or her personal juice with positive energy, perhaps by stating a brief affirmation. Then, one by one, pour your juice into the pitcher and stir it three times using a clockwise motion.

When all the juices have been poured into the pitcher, state in unison:

"This special potion
Blessed by each one
Joins us together
The magick's begun."

Fill your glasses, then toast one another and the successful future of your circle and your spells. Drink the magick potion.

COLLECT INGREDIENTS FOR SPELLS

Collecting the components for spells and rituals can be a joint activity that includes all participants in the magickal working. Not only does this process get everyone involved from the very beginning, it stimulates your imagination and heightens your anticipation.

INGREDIENTS/TOOLS:
• Depends on the spell

BEST TIME TO PERFORM THE SPELL:
• Depends on the spell

After you've decided upon a spell and have determined which objects you'll need, each person agrees to acquire one or more of those objects. As you seek out the ingredients for your spell, focus your mind on the outcome and how it will benefit all concerned. In this way, you start the magick even before you combine the components you've collected. When you've gathered all the necessary items, go through the steps of cleansing your magickal space, consecrating it, casting a circle, etc. together.

BUILD A PERMANENT CIRCLE

If your group is likely to work together for a while, you may decide to create a permanent circle in which to perform your magick spells and rituals. Stonehenge is an example of an ancient stone circle that archaeologists believe may have been a ritual site. Labyrinths are excellent configurations for magickal work, too. You needn't build something so elaborate, however. Consider these possibilities:

• Collect stones and lay them out in a circle that's large enough for your group to work inside. You may want to place four larger stones at the four compass directions.

- Plant flowers, shrubs, etc. in a circle.
- Erect a low wooden fence to form a circle.
- Install metal or wooden posts and string lights between them to form a circle.
- Indoors, you can paint a circle on the floor (if household members and/or your landlord agree).

Position an altar in the center of the circle—or in another spot if the group prefers. Over time, you can add to your circle, if you wish, or decorate it seasonally. Use your imagination!

SPELL TO FIND A HOME

Perform this spell with everyone who will occupy the home you seek—this is a joint effort, and the place in which you live will be important to all of you. Not only will your collective energies increase multiplicatively, you'll also clarify your intentions by working together to strengthen the bond between you.

INGREDIENTS/TOOLS:
- Pencils, pens, or markers
- Magazine pictures
- Scissors
- Glue or tape
- Poster board

BEST TIME TO PERFORM THE SPELL:
- On the new moon

Either sketch the house you're looking for (if you have artistic ability) or find pictures that depict features you seek in your new home. Glue these illustrations to a poster board and hang it where you'll see it often. Add words, symbols, and other objects that you consider meaningful. The goal is to create a visual tool that focuses your minds on your desire. Make it vivid and detailed. Kids love doing this sort of thing and often come up with great ideas. The more energy you pour into your intention, the quicker it will materialize.

GEMSTONE CHAKRA SPELL

As you learned in Chapter 2, the chakras are energy centers that run from the base of your spine to the top of your head. When they're balanced, you feel better physically, mentally, and emotionally. This spell uses the power of gemstones to help your chakras function harmoniously. Notice that the colors of the stones correspond to the colors associated with the 7 major chakras. Perform this spell with a friend or loved one.

INGREDIENTS/TOOLS:
- 1 piece of red jasper
- 1 piece of carnelian
- 1 piece of topaz
- 1 piece of jade
- 1 piece of aquamarine
- 1 piece of lapis lazuli
- 1 piece of amethyst

BEST TIME TO PERFORM THE SPELL:
- Anytime

Wash the stones with mild soap and water, then pat them dry. Find a comfortable place where you can lie down on your back undisturbed for about half an hour. Your partner in this spell first puts the red jasper on your pubic bone. Next, he or she sets the carnelian on your lower abdomen, about a hand's width below your belly button. The topaz goes on your solar plexus; the jade on the center of your chest near your heart; the aquamarine at the base of your throat; the lapis lazuli on your forehead, between your eyebrows. Finally, your partner places the amethyst so it touches the crown of your head.

Relax and sense the stones sending their healing vibrations into your body's energy centers, restoring harmony and well-being to your entire system. When you feel ready, ask your partner to remove the stones. Wash and dry the stones again. Swap places, so that now your partner is the recipient and you are the one positioning the stones on his or her body. After you've finished, cleanse the stones and store them in a safe place until you want to use them again.

THE MAGICK BOX

Everyone in the household—family members, roommates, romantic partners—can participate in this spell. You'll need a shoebox or a similar container that's small enough to fit on a shelf, but large enough to accommodate lots of wishes. This spell offers you a way to combine your energies to help all your wishes come true.

INGREDIENTS/TOOLS:
- 1 box with a lid
- Colored pens, pencils, or markers
- Magazine pictures, colored paper, stickers, other decorations
- Glue
- Slips of paper

BEST TIME TO PERFORM THE SPELL:
- During the waxing moon

Decorate the box however you like, using positive designs that appeal to you. Write words and/or symbols on it. Draw pictures. Affix images from magazines or downloaded from the Internet. The point is to personalize the box and to have fun engaging in the creative experience. On the top, write the words *The Magick Box.*

Put the box in place where everyone in your home has access to it and can see it when they enter the house or apartment. When the box is completely decorated, ask each member of the group to write 1 wish on a slip of paper and read it aloud to the others. Place the wishes in the box. Sharing your wishes with each other galvanizes your collective power. This builds momentum and attracts what you want more quickly. As each wish comes true, remove it from the box. Then make another wish and slip it into the box.

SPELL TO CALL IN DEITIES

This spell allows members of a group to call upon the guidance of the archangels: Raphael, Michael, Gabriel, and Uriel. You may petition their assistance in general, or ask for help with a particular issue.

INGREDIENTS/TOOLS:
- Sage incense
- Incense burner
- Matches or a lighter
- A few drops of the essential oil that corresponds to your issue; for general assistance, use sandalwood
- 1 ounce (or more if necessary) of a carrier oil, such as olive or grape seed, in a small dish
- 1 white pillar candle
- 1 nail, empty ballpoint pen, nail file, or other sharp object for carving the candle
- 1 cauldron (or fireproof bowl or saucer)
- 1 hand drum (optional)

BEST TIME TO PERFORM THE SPELL:
- As needed (see Chapter 8)

After forming your circle, set the sage incense in its holder on your altar and light it, thereby cleansing your working space. Add a few drops of the essential oil into the carrier oil and stir with your finger. Anoint each member of the circle by drawing a pentagram on his or her forehead with the oil (make sure no one in the group is allergic to the oil you've chosen). Ask each person in the circle to "sign" the candle by making a mark (word, sigil, astrological glyph, etc.) on the candle with the sharp implement. When everyone has finished inscribing the candle, rub the remaining oil on it (not on the wick), set it in the cauldron (or bowl or saucer) on your altar, and light the candle.

Have everyone focus on the candle's flame while you unify your energies toward your common objective. If someone opts to be the drummer, he or she should start beating a slow, steady rhythm now. Begin a low hum involving all participants in order to gently raise the energy.

A member of the group (chosen beforehand) takes the candle from the altar and holds it up, while facing east, and says:

"Raphael, bless this circle with your guidance. Help us to do right for those in need, and to work only for good."

Pass the candle to another member of the circle (chosen beforehand). This person faces south, holds up the candle, and says:

"Michael, bless this circle with your passion and strength. Help us to defend those in need, and to protect ourselves and our loved ones at all times and in all situations."

Pass the candle to another member of the circle (chosen beforehand). This person faces west, holds up the candle, and says:

"Gabriel, bless this circle with your love and serenity. Help us to bring light, love, and peace to those in need."

Pass the candle to another member of the circle (chosen beforehand). This person faces north, holds up the candle, and says:

"Uriel, bless this circle with your stability. Help us to provide comfort and healing for those in need."

Place the pillar candle on the altar again. While everyone in the circle focuses on the candle, say together:

"Behold, we summon the light of Spirit to guide this circle."

Allow time for everyone to gaze at the candle as it burns and flickers, opening your minds to visions, sensations, and guidance. Spend as much time as you need, or decide beforehand to end the spell after a certain amount of time has passed. At that time, a person selected in advance snuffs out the candle and releases the angelic presences (as described in Chapter 7).

Afterward, all members of the group sit together and discuss what they witnessed, thought, sensed, or otherwise gleaned from the session. This joint experience lets you gain insights from the higher realms regarding how to handle a particular matter or how to proceed with your magickal work.

CHOOSE YOUR TOTEM ANIMAL

Although we often associate totem animals with Native American tribes, clans throughout history and around the world have honored totem creatures and relied upon their assistance for protection, sustenance, and healing. Your spellworking circle may also benefit from the guidance of one or more totems.

INGREDIENTS/TOOLS:
- Book or list that describes spirit animals (such as my book *The Secret Power of Spirit Animals*)
- Paper
- Scissors
- Colored markers

BEST TIME TO PERFORM THE SPELL
- Anytime

Discuss the animals, birds, etc. with which you feel a strong affinity. Describe the characteristics of these creatures with which you resonate. You'll likely find that some members of the group identify with the same creatures. Also talk about the objectives you've set for your group, the path you intend to take, and/or what energies unite you. A frank discussion of this type will help you determine which animal guides are working with you—and which ones you wish to ask to assist you.

Try to narrow down your list of affiliate spirit animals to one, or at least no more than three. When everyone agrees on the totem(s) you want to work with, cut squares of paper for each person in your circle to draw images of the creature(s) you've elected as your group's totem(s). These images can be simple or elaborate, stylized or realistic—it's up to you. Carry these images with you or post them in a place where you'll see them often, so you can call upon the animal's energy whenever you need it.

Alternate suggestions: If you feel *really* dedicated and convinced that the creature(s) chosen are your lifelong totem(s), you may wish to have an image tattooed on your body. If you prefer a less painful (and less permanent) expression, draw the animal's image on your body with a marker.

HONORING YOUR SPIRIT ANIMAL TOTEM

This spell expands upon the previous one. It deepens your connection to your group's totem and to one another.

INGREDIENTS/TOOLS:
- Offerings for your totem animal
- 1 white pillar candle in a fireproof holder
- Matches or a lighter
- Individual candles, one for each member of the group (choose your preferred colors)

BEST TIME TO PERFORM THE SPELL:
- Anytime

As a group, shop for a figurine, wall hanging, or other image of your animal(s). Everyone should agree on the image you choose. Display the image on your altar or in another place of power where you meet to do spellwork. Place the white pillar candle in its holder on the altar and have one person light it. Say aloud as a group:

"Spirit guardian and guide
Now we seek your presence here.
Bring us wisdom from above
Fill us with your boundless love
And remain forever near."

Each person now steps up to the altar, one at a time, and first lays his or her offering before the image of your group totem, then lights his or her personal candle from the white pillar candle. If you have a specific request for your spirit guardian at this time, state it. If you wish to perform an additional spell or ritual at this time, go ahead. Otherwise, simply remain in this circle of light for as long as you choose, embracing the energy of your totem and the group. Then thank your totem and extinguish your candles.

Greet your group's totem each time you meet and before you perform a spell or ritual together, and thank it after you've finished.

INTIMACY LOTION

Does your lover seem distant lately? Is your sex life less fulfilling than usual? Are you often too busy or too tired to engage in true intimacy? Use this magick lotion with your partner to stimulate the senses, deepen your connection, and generate loving feelings between you.

INGREDIENTS/TOOLS:
- 1 copper bowl
- 1 spoon (silver or silver plate, if possible)
- 1 glass or china container with a lid (ideally the container should be pink or red, and/or decorated with designs that represent love to you, such as roses or hearts)
- Unscented massage oil or lotion
- A few drops of essential oils of rose, jasmine, ylang-ylang, patchouli, and/or musk—choose the scents you like: one, two, or all of them

BEST TIME TO PERFORM THE SPELL:
- During the waxing moon, preferably on a Friday

Wash the bowl, spoon, and container with mild soap and water. Pour the massage oil or lotion into the copper bowl. Add a few drops of one of the essential oils you've chosen. Using the silver spoon, stir the mixture, making three clockwise circles. Add a few drops of the second essential oil (if you've opted to include more than one). Again, make three clockwise circles to stir the blend. Repeat this process each time you add an essential oil. As you work, envision a beautiful pink light running from your heart to your lover's heart, growing to envelop you both in its radiant glow. After you've finished, pour the lotion/oil into the glass/china container and put the lid on.

Choose a time and place where you and your partner can spend an extended period of time together, undisturbed. Take turns massaging each other with the magick lotion. Relax and engage your senses. Allow the soothing touch and fragrant oils to enhance the connection between you.

LOVE POTION

After a while, many couples find that their relationships feel a little flat—like champagne without the bubbles. This spell pumps romance back into your partnership. Perform it with your beloved.

INGREDIENTS/TOOLS:
- 2 rose-colored candles in candleholders
- Matches or a lighter
- Sparkling apple cider or champagne
- 1 chalice (or pretty wine glass)

BEST TIME TO PERFORM THE SPELL:
- During the waxing moon, preferably on a Friday or when the sun and/or moon is in Libra

Set the candles on your altar (or a table, mantel, or other flat surface). Light one candle yourself and let your lover light the other. Pour the cider or champagne into your chalice. Share the drink, passing the chalice back and forth, while you focus on your desire for one another. If you wish, express your loving feelings for each other. After you've finished the drink, extinguish the candles. Repeat whenever you like.

Chapter 16

SEASONAL SPELLS AND MAGICKAL RECIPES

For centuries, earth-honoring cultures have followed the sun's apparent passage through the sky. Our ancestors divided the Wheel of the Year, as the sun's annual cycle is known, into eight periods of approximately six weeks each. As discussed in Chapter 8, each "spoke" corresponds to a particular degree in the zodiac. Wiccans and other pagans call these eight holidays (or holy days) "sabbats." It's no coincidence that many of our modern-day holidays fall close to these ancient, solar dates. Each of these special days affords unique opportunities for performing spells and rituals—the cosmic forces operating on these dates can increase the power of your magick.

Any day that holds special meaning for you can also be a good time for spellwork. Your birthday, for instance, is one of the most auspicious dates in the year for doing spells.

FOOD AND THE SEASONAL CYCLE

In our global village society, we can eat strawberries in January and tomatoes in November. We've forgotten that once upon a time people had to seize the opportunity to enjoy seasonal foods because they were only available for a short period of time. As different fruits and vegetables ripened, our ancestors were reminded of the changing seasons and their own place in nature's cycle.

You can explore the seasonal and spiritual aspects of food today by shopping regularly at a farmers' market. Week by week, the produce available will vary in supply and quality. By familiarizing yourself with what is in season at different times of the year in your region, you can gain a better understanding of how earth and cosmic energies influence the food you eat. In this way, preparing and ingesting food becomes a magickal experience, a way to align yourself with the Wheel of the Year and interact with the energies around you. Honor the spiritual force in the food you eat by acknowledging the consciousness that exists within all living substances and your connection with other life forms.

Blessing Hearth and Home

Food preparation takes on special meaning when you see each step of the process as magickal. As you cook and clean, use affirmations to bless your home and loved ones.

1. When you open the kitchen door say: "May only health, love, and joy come through this door into this home."

2. While stirring a pot say: "Thanks be to all beings who contributed to this meal."

3. While serving food say: "May the food I prepare nourish my loved ones in both body and soul."

4. While sweeping say: "May all harmful, disruptive, or unbalanced energy be removed from this place."

5. When you turn off the kitchen light at night say: "Bless this kitchen, and keep those of us who use it safe and healthy through the night."

HOLIDAY FOODS AND BEVERAGES

Our holiday celebrations usually include food and libation of some sort. We even associate certain foods with certain holidays—it just wouldn't be Thanksgiving without a turkey, for example. Most people don't realize, however, that fruits, vegetables, and other edibles contain magickal properties. You can combine them for specific purposes—in the same way you combine various ingredients to make amulets and talismans. Modern-day witches generally prefer soups, stews, and other "brews" made with ordinary food items instead of eye of newt and toe of frog, and in this chapter, you'll find a number of delicious magickal recipes you can enjoy at your holiday gatherings, in addition to other spells.

MAGICKAL FRUITS

Apple: love, health, longevity

Banana: fertility, strength

Blackberry: prosperity, protection, abundance

Blueberry: tranquility, peace, protection, prosperity

Cranberry: protection, healing

Grape: prosperity, fertility

Kiwi: fertility, love

Lemon: purification, protection, health

Lime: happiness, purification, healing

Mango: spirituality, happiness

Melons: love, peace

Orange: joy, health, purification

Peach: spirituality, fertility, love, harmony

Pear: love, health, prosperity

Pineapple: prosperity, luck, friendship

Plum: love, tranquility

Raspberry: strength, courage, healing (especially for women)

Strawberry: love, peace, happiness, luck

MAGICKAL VEGETABLES

Beans: love, family harmony

Broccoli: protection, abundance

Cabbage: prosperity

Carrot: fertility, healing (especially for men)

Cauliflower: fertility, protection

Celery: peace, concentration, mental clarity, health
Cucumber: fertility, healing
Garlic: protection, banishing, purification
Green pepper: prosperity
Lettuce: peace, harmony
Mushroom: strength, courage, protection
Onion: protection, exorcism, healing
Peas: love, abundance
Potato: fertility, abundance
Squash: abundance, harmony (consider the color/shape to understand correspondences)
Tomato: love, passion
MAGICKAL GRAINS
Barley: love, fertility
Corn: spirituality, security, prosperity, protection
Rice: fertility, happiness, love, protection
Rye: love, joy, affection
Wheat: strength, growth, abundance, success

Steps for Successful Spellcasting

Whenever you cast a spell, remember to use a few tried-and-true measures, as described in Chapter 1. These precautions can help you avoid complications, mix-ups, delays, or disappointments:

1. Remove all distractions.
2. Collect the ingredients and tools you'll use in your spell and cleanse them.
3. Purify and sanctify your space.
4. Quiet your mind.
5. Cast a circle around the area where you'll do your spellworking.
6. Perform the spell.
7. If you've called upon deities or spirits to assist you, thank and release them.
8. Open the circle.
9. Store your tools in a safe place until you need them again.

SAMHAIN CHILI

In many places, this sabbat coincides with deer-hunting season, so you may choose to make this delicious chili with venison rather than beef. Cooking this chili outdoors in an iron cauldron over a fire gives an added sense of magick and connection to the earth. Serve with cornbread or your favorite hearty whole-grain bread.

SERVES 6

INGREDIENTS/TOOLS:
- 4–6 large portobello mushrooms
- Bowl
- Red wine (approximately 1 cup, or more to taste)
- Large pot or iron cauldron
- Olive oil
- 2 onions, sliced
- 2 pounds ground beef or venison
- 2 (14½-ounce) cans diced tomatoes

- 1 (6-ounce) can tomato paste
- 2 (15-ounce) cans red kidney beans (or two cans mixed beans)
- Chili powder or dried chilies, to taste
- 2 bay leaves
- Salt and pepper, to taste
- Cheddar cheese, grated (optional)

BEST TIME TO MAKE THIS MAGICKAL MEAL:
- The evening of October 31

1. Chop the portobello mushrooms into small pieces, approximately ½" square, and place them in a mixing bowl.
2. Pour the red wine over the mushrooms. Allow to marinate in the refrigerator for at least 2 hours. Stir occasionally to make sure all the mushrooms have been marinated in the wine.
3. In a large pot or cauldron, heat the olive oil. Add the sliced onions, and cook until fragrant and soft. Add ground beef or venison, and cook until browned. Spoon off the fat. Stir in the tomatoes and tomato paste, then add the beans. Pour in the mushrooms and red wine and combine. Add the chilies and bay leaves. Adjust seasoning to taste, and add more red wine (or water) if desired.
4. Simmer for at least 3 hours. If desired, sprinkle grated sharp Cheddar on top of each bowl of chili before serving.

SPELL TO SEE THE FUTURE

Because the veils between the seen and unseen worlds are thinnest on Samhain, many witches and wizards practice divination at this time. This spell lets you glimpse the future and perhaps receive guidance from the other side.

INGREDIENTS/TOOLS:
- 1 black candle in a candleholder
- Matches or a lighter
- 1 tarot deck

- The evening of October 31

Quiet your mind, then light the candle and put it on your altar or another place where it can burn safely. Shuffle the tarot deck as you set an intention to receive guidance about the future. Select a card. Place the card face up in front of the candle. Take a few moments—or as long as you wish—to look at the card, allowing any impressions or insights to arise into your awareness. Try not to think of any preconceptions you may hold about this card's meaning—allow your intuition to speak to you.

Gaze at the candle's flame and let the flickering light calm your mind even further. Stare at the flame for as long as you wish, as visions, signals, sensations, emotions, etc. rise to the surface of your consciousness. You may notice a guardian spirit communicating with you. Ideas might pop into your mind that aren't like anything you've considered before. Let yourself glimpse impressions of the future, without apprehension. Continue for as long as you wish. When you feel ready, extinguish the candle and write down your experiences in your Book of Shadows.

YULE GOOD LUCK CHARM

Would you like to give your friends and loved ones the gift of good luck in the coming year? This Yuletide custom lets you make a unique magickal gift for everyone on your list.

INGREDIENTS/TOOLS:
- 1 Yule log (traditionally oak)
- Matches or a lighter
- Cloth drawstring pouches (1 for each person on your gift list)
- Dried pink rose petals (for love)
- Dried lavender flowers (for peace of mind)
- Dried basil (for protection)
- Dried mint leaves (for prosperity)
- Dried echinacea (for health)
- 1 sheet of paper

- Scissors
- 1 pen

BEST TIME TO PERFORM THE SPELL:
- Yule (usually December 21)

On the night of the winter solstice, build a Yule fire in a safe place and burn an oak log in it. Allow the fire to burn down completely. The next morning after the ashes have cooled, scoop some into each pouch. Add the dried botanicals. Cut the sheet of paper into slips, so you have one for each person on your list. Write a personalized wish on each slip of paper. Fold the papers three times and add them to the pouches. Tie the pouches closed, bless them, and give them to your loved ones.

HOLIDAY PROTECTION WREATH

Holidays can be stressful times, even under the best of circumstances. This special table wreath does double duty—it serves as a pretty decoration while emitting good vibes to protect your sanity during the hectic holiday season.

INGREDIENTS/TOOLS:
- 1 piece of cardboard or poster board
- Scissors
- Lots of dried bay leaves
- Tacky glue, double-sided tape, or other fixative
- 1 white pillar candle in a glass holder
- Matches or a lighter

BEST TIME TO PERFORM THE SPELL:
- As needed

Cut a circle from the cardboard or poster board, then cut a hole in the center to make a "donut" large enough to slip over the candle in its holder. Like all circles, this one is a symbol of protection. Attach the bay leaves to the cardboard circle to make a wreath. Think peaceful thoughts as you work. Position the candle on your table, altar, or mantel. Slide the bay leaf wreath over it, so it circles the base of the candle. Light the candle and gaze into its flame to relax your mind and calm your nerves.

BRIGID'S CROSS

The Celtic goddess Brigid is associated with creativity, fertility, smith-craft, and the hearth. Often, she's depicted stirring a cauldron over dancing flames—both symbols of creativity. You can celebrate Brigid's Day (also known as Imbolc and Candlemas) by fashioning what's known as Crios Bridghe or Brigid's Cross, even though it's really a circle. Jumping through the magick circle brings good fortune.

INGREDIENTS/TOOLS:
- Scissors or pruning shears
- 3 vines or lengths of raffia (available in crafts stores), each 5 feet long
- 2 pieces of white cord or ribbon

BEST TIME TO PERFORM THE SPELL:
- Between January 31 and February 2

Cut the vines or raffia. Think of 3 wishes you want to come true, and assign 1 wish to each vine or length of raffia. Tie the vines or raffia together with 1 piece of cord or ribbon. Braid the vines/raffia, focusing on your wishes as you work. When you reach the end, tie the braid with the other piece of cord/ribbon. Then bend the braid around to form a circle and tie the 2 pieces of cord/ribbon together, making 3 knots. Lay the circle on the ground or floor, and step into it. Then lift the circle up along your body and over your head as you imagine yourself receiving the 3 wishes you desire. Hang the wreath in your home to bring blessings your way.

OSTARA SPELL TO BIRTH A NEW PROJECT

Are you having a hard time getting a project off the ground? Do delays, deterrents, and disappointments keep interfering with your progress?

This spell "fertilizes" your idea and helps you bring your venture to fruition. The custom of painting eggs at Easter originated with the early festival of Ostara, which is held on the spring equinox. Eggs are symbols of birth, life, and fertility, and Ostara celebrates the Earth's renewal after the long, cold winter.

INGREDIENTS/TOOLS:
- 1 raw egg
- 1 straight pin or needle
- 1 bowl
- Acrylic or watercolor paints
- 1 small paintbrush
- Water

BEST TIME TO PERFORM THE SPELL:
- On the Spring Equinox

Gently wash the egg first to remove bacteria as well as unwanted energies. Carefully poke a hole in each end of the egg with a pin. Holding the egg above the bowl, place your mouth over one hole, and gently blow the contents of the egg out through the other hole. When you've finished, rinse out the eggshell and let it dry.

Paint symbols and images on the eggshell that represent your project, as well as your objectives. Consider including colors, numbers, runes, astrological glyphs, and other symbols that relate to your intentions. Make sure everything you include has positive connotations for you. While you work, visualize your project moving forward and receiving the support and recognition you seek. See your goals coming to fruition, your success assured. You don't have to understand all the steps between the inception of your idea and its fulfillment; just imagine the end result you desire coming true.

After you've finished decorating your egg, display it on your altar or in a place where you'll see it often. Each time you look at it, you'll be reminded of your goal and your intention to succeed. Alternate suggestion: Hard-boil the egg. After the egg has cooled, decorate it. As you paint the egg and as you eat it, focus on your goal; see yourself achieving it happily. Save the eggshell pieces to use in another spell.

SEASONAL POTPOURRI

Dry potpourri blends the energies and fragrances of herbs, flowers, and spices for sensory and magickal purposes. You can place an open dish of potpourri in a room to scent the air and to draw, enhance, or disperse energies according to your will. Don't chop up your plant material—if you intend to dry fresh botanicals yourself for your potpourri, try to keep them as unbruised as possible, as the natural oils give flowers and spices their scent. When dry, crumble the plant matter into chunks.

INGREDIENTS/TOOLS:

- Glass bowl
- Dried herbs, flowers, and spices—your choice, depending on your intentions and the season
- Powdered orris root (2 tablespoons orris root powder per cup of dry potpourri mix)
- Essential oil(s)—your choice, depending on your intentions and the season (6 drops of essential oil per cup of dry mix)

BEST TIME TO PERFORM THE SPELL:

- Anytime

Place all the dried plant matter (including the powdered orris root) in a bowl and stir with your hands to combine. Sprinkle with the essential oil and stir again. Keep the blend in a closed container for at least 2 weeks so it can mellow; this allows the scents to blend. Open the container and stir it once a day to keep it from going moldy. Even if you think your plant material is perfectly dry, sometimes a drop or two of moisture may be left in it. When it's ready, put your potpourri in an open container and place it in the area you wish to be affected by the energy. It's also a nice idea to set a small amount of potpourri in a dish on your altar as an offering to deities.

Don't forget about your dry potpourri once you've set it out. Dust collects in it, and exposure to air and the energy of the room will eventually weaken the herbal components. Make a new batch when you feel that the vitality of the old one has expired. You can bury used potpourri, add it to ritual fires, or compost it. Dry potpourri also makes a good stuffing for herbal pillows, sachets, and poppets.

BELTANE TALISMAN TO ATTRACT LOVE

This ancient spring festival is held on May 1, and celebrates love, sexuality, pleasure, and fertility. At this time in the Wheel of the Year, the earth is ripe with nature's beauty—flowers blossom, leaves appear on the trees, baby animals and birds are born. Not surprisingly, this is the ideal time to perform love spells.

INGREDIENTS/TOOLS:
- 2 pieces of red felt, about 4 inches square
- Scissors
- 1 piece of paper
- 1 pen
- 1 penny
- 1 seashell
- 1 small elongated stone
- Needle and red thread

BEST TIME TO PERFORM THE SPELL:
- The morning of May 1

Imagine that one piece of felt represents you and the other represents your partner. Fold one piece of felt in half and, using the scissors, cut out one lobe of a heart shape starting from the folded edge. Then cut the other piece of felt in the same manner. On the piece of paper, write words and draw pictures or symbols that symbolize love—as many as you can, until you've filled the entire piece of paper. Wrap the paper tightly around the penny (copper is linked with Venus, the planet and goddess of love). Lay the penny, shell, and stone between the two felt hearts. Sew them together, envisioning the two hearts becoming one. Sleep with the charm under your pillow until your love manifests.

SPRINGTIME SMOOTHIE

You've heard the expression "You are what you eat," right? For this spell, you choose the fruits and/or veggies (from the table at the beginning of this chapter) that represent things you want to incorporate into yourself—all living things embody energy and they influence your own energy when you ingest them.

INGREDIENTS/TOOLS:
- Fruits/veggies that contain the magickal qualities you desire (organic if possible)
- 1 paring knife
- Blender
- Fruit/vegetable juice that contains the magickal qualities you desire
- Plain yogurt

BEST TIME TO PERFORM THIS SPELL:
- On the morning of May 1

Before you begin, wash all the fruits you've chosen and pat them dry. Then close your eyes and hold your hands palms-down above the fruit. Feel the energy radiating from the fruit; sense your connection with the fruits you've chosen. State aloud that both the nutrients and the magickal components contained in the fruit you've selected will benefit you in every way. Cut the fruit into small pieces and put them into the blender. Add the fruit juice, as much as you need to create the consistency you like. Then add as much yogurt as you like and blend everything until smooth. As you drink the magickal smoothie you've concocted, envision it bringing you good fortune and fulfilling your desires.

Alternate suggestion: If you prefer, combine the fruits/veggies you've chosen for a refreshing salad. Then add a dollop of yogurt and sprinkle with the petals from edible flowers, such as violets or nasturtiums, that represent your intentions.

MIDSUMMER CANDLE SPELL FOR GOOD FORTUNE

On Midsummer (the summer solstice), daylight in the Northern Hemisphere is longer than at any other time of the year. Therefore, candles—which symbolize the fire element and the sun—often play a role in spells and rituals performed on this sabbat. Fire also represents the masculine force in the universe, whereas water represents the feminine force. This easy spell combines both elements to bring good fortune and balance into your life.

INGREDIENTS/TOOLS:
- 1 floating candle in a color that represents a particular wish or desire (see the color correspondence charts at the beginnings of earlier chapters), or choose a golden-yellow candle to signify the sun
- Matches or a lighter

BEST TIME TO PERFORM THE SPELL:
- Midsummer's Eve

Take your candle and matches or lighter to a body of water—a gently flowing stream, a pond or lake, a quiet ocean cove. With your intention, empower the candle to bring you whatever you seek—love, money, success, etc. Say aloud:

"I shine this light
Into the night,
The power of fire
Attracts my desire."

Set the candle in the water, keeping your intention clearly in your mind, and watch the flame until it burns down or the water extinguishes it.

"There are two ways of spreading light: to be
The candle or the mirror that reflects it."
　　　　　　　　—EDITH WHARTON, "VESALIUS IN ZANTE. (1564)"

SUMMER SOLSTICE GAZPACHO

This chilled vegetable soup is a refreshing, healthy summer solstice treat. Green peppers signify prosperity; cucumber is associated with peace, harmony, and health; tomatoes and avocados attract love; celery encourages peace; onions and garlic provide protection and health.

SERVES 8–10

INGREDIENTS/TOOLS:

- Blender
- 2 large green bell peppers, cored, seeded, and diced
- 1 large cucumber, peeled and chopped
- 2 pounds tomatoes, cored and diced
- 1 celery stalk, chopped
- 1 onion, chopped
- 2 garlic cloves, peeled
- 1 avocado, chopped (optional)
- 1 large glass bowl
- 1 teaspoon salt
- ¼ teaspoon cayenne pepper
- Pinch of basil
- Pinch of parsley
- ⅓ cup olive oil
- 1 tablespoon lemon juice
- ¼ cup red wine vinegar
- 2 cans (12- or 15-ounce) tomato juice
- Sour cream, plain yogurt, fresh cilantro as a garnish, and/or corn or tortilla chips (optional)

1. In a blender, combine the first seven ingredients in small batches and blend until smooth. Pour into a large bowl. Add seasonings, oil, lemon juice, vinegar, and tomato juice and stir well to combine. Cover and chill for at least 5 hours or overnight.
2. Stir well and taste before serving. Adjust seasonings as necessary. Serve in bowls or large mugs. Garnish the soup as desired with sour cream or yogurt, fresh cilantro, and/or corn or tortilla chips.

SEASONAL COLLAGES

The whole family can engage in this magick spell. Young children love participating. You can make one collage for each season, or choose holidays throughout the year that you'd like to recognize. You can make your collage any size, but if you use a 22" × 28" poster board you'll have plenty of room for images and found objects.

INGREDIENTS/TOOLS:
- Scissors
- Pictures from magazines, flyers, catalogs, old greeting cards, photographs; images downloaded from the Internet
- Crayons, markers, colored pencils
- Blank drawing paper or construction paper
- Glue
- Poster board (whatever color you like, or connect it to the season: green for spring, orange for fall)
- Found objects related to the season (seashells, pinecones, leaves, flower petals, etc.)

BEST TIME TO PERFORM THE SPELL:
- At the change of the season

Cut out images associated with the season (summer-themed images might include beach umbrellas, ice cream, swimming pools, sandals, the sun, and so forth). Draw pictures or write words on the blank paper and cut them out as well. Glue the images and words to the poster board. You may lay the images out first to find a pattern that pleases you, or you can begin gluing the images wherever you feel inspired and allow the collage to form on its own. Then attach "found" objects to the collage. Take the collage down at the end of a holiday or season and begin the next collage. If you wish, date and store your collages, or burn them in a ritual fire to symbolize releasing the past from your life in preparation for what's upcoming.

Alternate suggestion: You can explore themes or ideas that are meaningful to you through this collaging project. For example, create an ancestor collage that looks at your family's heritage and its ways of celebrating holidays, bringing in traditions from the countries and cultures of your past.

LUGHNASADH PEASANT BREAD

Corn, wheat, and other grains are typically harvested around Lughnasadh, the holiday of the Celtic god Lugh. In agrarian cultures, this was the time to begin preparing for the barren winter months that lay ahead. Our ancestors cut, ground, and stored grain, canned fruit and vegetables, and brewed wine and beer in late summer. In addition to making this ritual bread, you might want to consider brewing your own beer, too.

MAKES 1 LOAF

INGREDIENTS/TOOLS:
- Small bowl
- 3 tablespoons sugar, divided
- 1 cup warm water (around 110°F), divided
- 2 heaping teaspoons yeast (or one package)
- Large bowl
- 2 cups flour (with more for kneading)
- 1 tablespoon finely chopped fresh rosemary
- 1 tablespoon finely chopped fresh thyme
- 1 tablespoon finely chopped fresh dill
- 1 tablespoon finely chopped fresh chives
- Olive oil
- 1 clean cloth
- Baking sheet

BEST TIME TO PERFORM THE SPELL:
- August 1

1. In a small bowl, stir 1 teaspoon of sugar into ¼ cup of warm water. Sprinkle the yeast over the top and allow it to proof until foamy (about 5 minutes).
2. In a large bowl, stir the remaining sugar into the flour. Make a well in the flour and pour the yeast in. Add the herbs and 1 tablespoon olive oil to the flour mixture. Stir to combine all the ingredients.

The Modern Witchcraft Spell Book

3. Slowly add the warm water as you stir to create a firm dough ball. If you add too much water, simply add a bit of flour to compensate. Scrape the sides of the bowl and add the scrapings to the dough ball.
4. Sprinkle the ball and bowl with a bit of flour. Cover with a clean cloth and set to rise in a warm place with no drafts until the dough has doubled in size (approximately an hour and a half).
5. Remove the dough from bowl and place on a floured surface. Knead for approximately 5 minutes until smooth and elastic. Sprinkle flour onto the kneading surface as necessary so that the dough does not stick.
6. Form the dough into a loaf-shaped log. Place on the baking sheet or in a bread pan. Brush the entire top with olive oil and leave to rise to the height you desire. (Placing the dough in a barely warm oven is a good place for it to rise.) Heat the oven to 400°F. (If your bread is rising in the oven, remove it carefully and then heat the oven.) Bake the bread for 30–40 minutes, or until golden brown.

Alternate suggestion: Choose herbs for specific purposes: onion for protection, poppy seeds for happiness and insight, etc. See the table at the beginning of this chapter for a list of vegetables and their associations.

SPELL TO BLESS THE EARTH

In keeping with the traditional harvest theme of Lughnasadh, this spell uses corn, wheat, or straw in a ritual blessing for Mother Earth and to give thanks for her bounty. It also marks the decline of the sun's power as the Wheel of the Year turns toward winter.

INGREDIENTS/TOOLS:
- Dried corn leaves, straw, wheat, or another grain
- Scissors
- Twine (made from a natural fabric, not plastic or nylon)
- 1 large iron cauldron (optional)
- Matches or a lighter

BEST TIME TO PERFORM THE SPELL:
- August 1

Fashion the dried corn leaves (or other grain) into a humanlike shape to represent the Sun King, whose powers are now waning. Cut pieces of twine and tie it around the "corn doll" to form its head, arms, and legs. Trim as needed. Build a fire in your cauldron, fireplace, or other safe spot. Burn the doll in the fire as an offering to Mother Earth.

MABON SOUP

Serve this lovely soup on the autumn equinox, also called Mabon. Apples are associated with love, health, protection, and immortality—cut one in half, and you'll see that the seeds are configured as a star/pentagram. Almonds carry the energy of prosperity; curry offers strength and protection.

SERVES 4–6
INGREDIENTS / TOOLS:

- 1½ pounds apples
- Paring knife
- ¼ cup butter
- Large saucepan
- 1 onion, finely chopped
- 6 tablespoons ground almonds
- 4 cups chicken or vegetable stock
- ½ teaspoon curry powder
- Salt and freshly ground pepper, to taste
- Blender or food processor
- Strainer
- ½ cup light cream, plain yogurt, or almond milk
- Toasted sliced almonds for garnish

1. Core, peel, and dice the apples. Melt the butter in a saucepan. Add the onion and cook gently until softened (about 5 minutes). Add the apples and stir gently for 2–3 minutes. Sprinkle the ground almonds over the apple and onion mixture, and stir for another 1–2 minutes.
2. Pour in the stock and bring to a boil. Add the curry powder, and salt and pepper to taste.

The Modern Witchcraft Spell Book

3. Reduce the heat to low. Cover and simmer for 20 minutes. The apples should be tender.
4. Remove from the heat and allow to cool to room temperature. Pour the soup into the blender or food processor and blend until smooth.
5. Pour the soup through a strainer into a clean pan. Add the cream, yogurt, or almond milk and stir until blended. Taste for seasoning and adjust if necessary. If the soup is too thick, add a bit more stock. Reheat gently (don't boil). Serve hot, garnished with a few toasted sliced almonds and an additional pinch of curry powder on top, if you desire.

Chapter 17

MISCELLANEOUS SPELLS

Whatever your problem, concern, or desire, a spell probably exists to address it. If you can't find one that's exactly what you're looking for—or can't get your hands on the recommended ingredients—then create your own spell. In previous chapters you'll find tables of information about colors, gemstones, botanicals, and other ingredients that can add to the power of your spells. Use these suggestions, if you wish, to customize your spell.

Steps for Successful Spellcasting

Whenever you cast a spell, remember to use a few tried-and-true measures, as described in Chapter 1. These precautions can help you avoid complications, mix-ups, delays, or disappointments:

1. Remove all distractions.
2. Collect the ingredients and tools you'll use in your spell and cleanse them.
3. Purify and sanctify your space.
4. Quiet your mind.
5. Cast a circle around the area where you'll do your spellworking.
6. Perform the spell.
7. If you've called upon deities or spirits to assist you, thank and release them.
8. Open the circle.
9. Store your tools in a safe place until you need them again.

GOOD VIBRATIONS POTION

Virtually any place can benefit from this uplifting spell. Do it when you move into a new home or after an argument or party, in your workplace, in your car—wherever you choose. It can even help boost your mood if you're feeling down in the dumps. Not only does it clear away unwanted vibrations, it fills your space with the fresh scent of oranges.

INGREDIENTS/TOOLS:
- 1 spray bottle (preferably made of clear glass)
- Saltwater
- A few drops of orange essential oil

BEST TIME TO PERFORM THE SPELL:
- Anytime

Fill the spray bottle with saltwater (if you don't live near the ocean, just add a pinch of sea salt to spring water). Add the essential oil and shake the bottle three times to charge the water. Start in the east and mist each room with this potion to clear away negative energy and fill the air with good vibrations.

ALADDIN'S LAMP

Remember the fable about the boy Aladdin who found a magick lamp with a genie inside? Like the genie in the story, this spell grants you 3 wishes.

INGREDIENTS/TOOLS:
• Metal oil lamp or a covered incense burner
• Incense
• Matches or a lighter

BEST TIME TO PERFORM THE SPELL:
• Depends on your wishes (see Chapter 8)

Use an old-fashioned oil lamp made of brass, tin, copper, or silver if you can find one; otherwise, substitute an incense burner with a lid that has perforations in it to allow the smoke to float out. Fit the incense into the lamp or incense burner and light it. Put the lid on so the smoke rises from the spout or perforations. Hold your hands on either side of the lamp or incense burner (don't actually touch it if the sides are hot) and pretend to rub it. Envision the smoke as a powerful genie who has come to do your bidding. You might even see a figure form in the smoke.

State your 3 wishes aloud as affirmations. In your mind's eye, see them already coming true. Spend a few minutes focusing on your requests as you inhale the scent of the incense. When you're ready, thank the "genie" for its assistance.

FEAR OF FLYING SPELL

Does the idea of soaring eight miles above the earth in a metal cylinder make you feel weak in your knees? And what about all those terrorist stories you keep hearing? What can you do to calm your fears of flying? One way is to enlist the aid of the air spirits, known as *sylphs*. Here's how.

INGREDIENTS/TOOLS:
- White carnation petals
- 1 container in which to carry the carnation petals
- Clove incense
- Incense burner
- Matches or a lighter
- 1 fan made of feathers (or a single large feather)

BEST TIME TO PERFORM THE SPELL:
- On a Wednesday or Thursday, at least a day before your trip

If possible, perform this spell outside. Pluck the petals from several white carnations and place them in a bowl or other container. Fit the incense into its burner and light it. Waft the smoke toward you with the fan (or use the feather and your hand to guide the smoke toward you). Turn around, allowing the smoke to touch all sides of your body. Tap both shoulders with the fan, then tap your body at the places where the seven main chakras or energy centers are located, starting at the crown chakra and ending at the root chakra.

Invite the sylphs to join you. Sylphs are nature elementals who serve as ambassadors of the element of air. You may see faint flickering lights or feel a shift in the air around you as they come to answer your call. They might even appear to you as tiny winged beings. Request their assistance on your trip. Express your concerns and explain what you would like them to do for you. Speak to them with courtesy and respect, as you would to a human being from whom you sought aid. Tell them you've brought a gift to thank them in advance for helping you. Open the container and scatter the carnation petals in the wind. You may notice that the wind picks up or changes direction as the sylphs accept your offering.

If you wish, take the fan or feather with you when you fly, to remind you that you are protected by the spirits of the air. Additional suggestion:

Wear the Gemstone Necklace for a Safe Trip (see Chapter 11) on your trip.

SPELL FOR A HAPPY HOME

If you live with other people, you may want to invite them to do this easy spell with you (if you think they'd be open to it). If you think they might object if they knew you were doing magick, you don't have to tell them—they'll just think you're decorating your home.

INGREDIENTS/TOOLS:
- Lavender-scented incense
- Incense burner
- Matches or a lighter
- Several houseplants with round leaves
- 1 wreath

BEST TIME TO PERFORM THE SPELL:
- Anytime

Fit the incense into the incense burner and place it near the front door of your home. Fragrant lavender dissolves stress and promotes serenity. Position the plants throughout your home. Put at least one in each room, and set one on your altar (if you have one). The round leaves represent harmony and unity. Jade plants are excellent choices because they also attract wealth, prosperity, and good health. Hang the wreath on your door to welcome positive forces into your home. Continue caring for your plants, watering and feeding them to keep them healthy. Periodically, light incense to keep positive energy wafting through your home.

Wreaths for All Seasons

Consider hanging a festive, seasonal wreath on your door and changing it at least four times a year. This practice keeps you in touch with the Earth's natural cycles. Changing the wreath periodically also prevents stagnation and draws new opportunities to you and the occupants of your home.

SPELL TO FIND A PARKING PLACE

It's the day after Thanksgiving, an icy rain is falling, and the mall parking lot is jammed with cars. You'd hoped to find a parking spot close to the entrance, but it looks like the nearest spaces are half a mile away. Don't worry; ask the parking goddess Barbara to come to your aid.

INGREDIENTS/TOOLS:
- None

BEST TIME TO PERFORM THE SPELL:
- Anytime

Stop driving around in circles, close your eyes, and take a few slow, deep breaths. In your mind's eye, see an empty space waiting for you exactly where you want to park. Recite this incantation aloud:

"Goddess Barbara, fair of face
Guide me to my parking place."

Open your eyes and drive to the spot the goddess has provided for you.

SPELL TO OVERCOME AN OBSTACLE

Anytime a daunting challenge faces you and you fear you don't have the strength to deal with it, call in some extra muscle to help you handle the task—magickally, that is. Since ancient times, the people of India have drawn upon the power of the elephant god Ganesh to help them overcome seemingly insurmountable obstacles. So can you.

INGREDIENTS/TOOLS:
- 1 image of an elephant or of Ganesh (for example, a small figurine or an image downloaded from the Internet)
- 1 athame (or table knife)

- On a Saturday, preferably during the waning moon, or when the sun or moon is in Capricorn

Close your eyes and imagine you're in a dark, dense jungle. The faintest light shines down through the branches high overhead and the vegetation is so thick you can see only a foot or two ahead of you. All sorts of dangers lurk unseen. Your situation seems impossible. You feel trapped and helpless.

Suddenly you hear the trumpeting call of an elephant—it's Ganesh coming to your rescue. Pick up your athame or table knife. Without hesitation he rushes toward you and easily lifts you with his trunk onto his back. Explain to him the nature of your problem. The tangled vines and thick overgrowth represent the obstacles facing you. Now visualize yourself riding on Ganesh's back as he marches into the jungle, trampling everything in his path.

Reach out with your athame and begin slashing away at the vines and branches in your way. Envision yourself hacking through the obstacles that blocked you before. See space opening up before you. Feel Ganesh's strength, lifting you high above your problems. Together you are unstoppable. Keep chopping away at the thick vegetation, eliminating obstacles one by one. You don't have to see all the way to the end, just tackle each conundrum as it presents itself. When you feel ready, climb down from Ganesh's back and thank him for his assistance. You now realize you have the ability to handle whatever challenges arise.

SPELL TO MANIFEST A TRIP YOU DESIRE

Is there someplace you've always wanted to go? Don't worry about how you'll get the money or time for the trip—just do your magick and let the universe handle the arrangements.

INGREDIENTS/TOOLS:

- Magazine photos or other images of places you want to go
- Maps, travel brochures, etc.
- Other symbols that represent travel to you

- Colored markers or pens
- 1 large sheet of heavy paper or cardboard
- Glue or tape
- Sandalwood incense
- Incense burner
- Matches or a lighter

BEST TIME TO PERFORM THE SPELL:
- During the waxing moon, preferably when the sun or moon is in Sagittarius, or on a Thursday

Collect pictures from magazines and travel catalogs of a place you'd like to visit. Gather maps, brochures, and other information about this place. Find symbols and images that represent travel to you—a toy airplane, a tiny boat, a hotel from a Monopoly game, seashells, and anything that relates to the trip you're planning.

After you've gathered as many things as you feel you need, use the markers to draw a circle on the piece of paper or cardboard—it should be large enough that you can stand within it. Glue or tape all the symbols you've collected inside the circle. Also inside the circle you can draw additional pictures and/or write words that describe your intentions, such as the names of the places you plan to visit or affirmations stating your desires.

When your "wish board" is finished, light the incense. Stand in the middle of the board and envision yourself journeying to the place(s) you've chosen. Make your visualization as clear and vivid as possible. Try to intuit the mood of the place, the sights, sounds, and smells. Enjoy yourself. Remain in the circle, imagining your journey, until the incense finishes burning.

TRAVEL POTION

To ensure that your trip goes smoothly, and that you enjoy yourself, make this magick travel potion before you leave home.

- 1 clear glass bottle
- Water
- The knight of wands from a tarot deck
- 1 red ribbon

BEST TIME TO PERFORM THE SPELL:

- On a Thursday, before your trip

Fill the bottle with water. Lay the knight of wands (the tarot card of travel and adventure) face up on your altar and set the bottle of water on the card. Leave it there overnight. In the morning, tie the red ribbon around the neck of the bottle, making 3 knots. As you tie each knot, repeat an affirmation such as "I enjoy a lovely, relaxing vacation" and visualize the end result in your mind's eye.

If you're driving, carry the bottle of magickally imprinted water with you on your trip. Sip the water periodically throughout the journey. If you're flying, drink the water before you go to the airport. As you drink, feel yourself having the perfect trip and a wonderful time away.

MILK OF HUMAN KINDNESS SPELL

This spell gives energy back to the earth—our home that gives so much to us. Do this balancing spell once a month, to keep positive energy flowing between you and the planet. It's also good to do whenever a wish has been granted or an important spell has succeeded, to show your gratitude.

INGREDIENTS/TOOLS:

- 1 small pot
- 1 cup milk
- 1 teaspoon honey
- A pinch of dried lavender flowers
- 1 clean glass jar
- 1 small moonstone

- At dawn or dusk, preferably when the sun or moon is in Taurus

In a small pot, warm the milk, the honey, and the lavender over low heat until the honey has dissolved—don't let it boil. Remove from the heat and it cool to room temperature. Pour the liquid into the jar. Touch the moonstone to your forehead, to your lips, then to your heart, and then add the stone gently to the liquid. Dip your finger into the milk, touch your heart with it, then dip your finger back into the liquid. Visualize the peace and gratitude in your heart being transferred to the milk.

Cap the jar and carry it outside to a tree near your home, or a tree that is special to you. Bow to the tree, uncap the jar, and pour the milk and the stone out at the base of the tree on the roots, as you say aloud:

> *"I give to the earth*
> *As the earth gives to me.*
> *Bless all who live here*
> *For eternity."*

Bow again to the tree, and feel loving energy flowing between you. If you wish, sit and meditate beneath the tree, or even climb up into its branches.

SO MUCH TO DO, SO LITTLE TIME

Does it seem that no matter how hard you work, you never seem to get caught up? If stress and frustration are getting you down, this spell offers a welcome respite from the demands the world makes on you.

INGREDIENTS/TOOLS:
- Lavender incense
- Incense burner
- 1 light blue candle
- 1 candleholder
- Matches or a lighter
- A bathtub full of comfortably hot water

The Modern Witchcraft Spell Book

- A few drops of vanilla essential oil
- 4 good-sized chunks of citrine

- Anytime

Fit the incense and candle in their respective holders, set them on your bathroom vanity, then light both. Fill the bathtub with water. Add several drops of vanilla essential oil to the bathwater. After washing the citrines with mild soap and water, set one at each corner of the bathtub. Climb into the tub and make yourself comfy. Feel the citrines—known for their clarifying ability—drawing off your stress and neutralizing it.

Feel your frustrations and anxieties dissolving into the bathwater. The trick is not to think about anything outside the walls of the bathroom. When you worry about the past or future, you block receptivity to new ideas and guidance that could help you resolve problems. If a troublesome thought pops into your mind, send it into the water or let the citrines dissolve it. Soak for as long as you like until you feel calm, rested, and confident that all is well.

When your peace of mind is restored, get out of the tub. As the water drains away, visualize your cares flowing away with it. Pick up the citrines and thank them. Then wash them with clean water (not the bathwater) and mild soap, and pat them dry. Allow the candle and incense to burn down safely.

DEITY ASSISTANCE SPELL

Are you faced with a challenging situation, and can't figure out how to handle it? Whatever your problem is, there's a deity who can help. This spell requests divine assistance through burning incense, which in some spiritual traditions is considered an offering to the deities. As the smoke rises, it carries your request into the heavens.

INGREDIENTS/TOOLS:
- A picture, figurine, or other image of your chosen deity
- Incense

- Incense burner
- Matches or a lighter
- 1 slip of paper
- 1 pen or pencil

- Depends on your intention (see Chapter 8)

Determine which deity is best suited to help you with your problem. (You'll find lots of information online and in books.) Then acquire an image/figurine of that god or goddess and display it on your altar. Select an incense that corresponds to your intentions—cinnamon or clove for career success, rose or jasmine for love, and so on. (See tables at the beginnings of Chapters 9–14.) Fit the incense into its burner and light it. Write your request on the slip of paper, fold it three times, and lay it at the feet of the deity.

Envision your request floating up to the heavens, carried on the incense smoke to your chosen god or goddess. Quiet your mind and listen for an answer or guidance. (Note: The answer may not come immediately—it could take a few days—so don't grow impatient.) Allow the incense to burn down completely. Thank the deity for helping you and trust that aid will come at the appropriate time.

CLEAR THE AIR

Have you ever wondered why witches use brooms? No, not for flying. Brooms sweep away disruptive energy from a space. Perform this cleansing ritual after an argument, a party, or anytime you feel a need to clear the air.

INGREDIENTS/TOOLS:
- 1 broom
- 1 bowl
- Saltwater
- Sage (bundled, loose, or incense)
- 1 fireproof holder that you can carry easily
- Matches or a lighter

• As needed

If possible, open the windows and doors. Start sweeping your home (or other space) with a broom—not just the floor, but the air as well. Wave the broom through the entire area, side to side, up and down, until you feel you've whisked away the psychic "dirt." Next, fill a small bowl with saltwater. Sprinkle a little in each corner of your home, then flick some water in the center of each room. Finally, put the sage into the holder and light it. Blow out the flames and let it smoke. Carry the burning sage from room to room, allowing its cleansing smoke to clear the air and restore peace to your home.

SPELL TO PERPETUATE POSITIVE ENERGY

We all hit rough spots in life, when it's hard to stay optimistic. If you're in one of those low periods, let this spell give you a boost. After you've done it once, you can cast the spell in an abbreviated form anytime, simply through the power of fragrance.

TOOLS/**I**NGREDIENTS:
• Music that lifts your mood
• A few drops of bay essential oil
• A few drops of frankincense essential oil
• A few drops of jasmine essential oil
• A few drops of eucalyptus essential oil
• 1 yellow candle in a holder
• 1 red candle in a holder
• 1 blue candle in a holder
• 1 green candle in a holder
• Matches or a lighter

BEST **TIME TO PERFORM THE SPELL:**
• On the new moon

The new moon is best for this spell because as the moon's light increases, so will your energy and optimism. But you can do this spell on any night, whenever you need a boost of positive energy. With your intent firmly in mind, put on your favorite uplifting music. Rub the essential oils on the candles (not on the wicks) in the order shown in the Ingredients/Tools list (bay oil on the yellow candle, frankincense on the red one, and so on).

Position the candles in the four cardinal points: yellow in the east, red in the south, blue in the west, green in the north. Light the candles in this order, casting a circle of light around you. Say aloud:

"I enter the flow of All That Is.
I am filled with loving kindness.
I release all negative and unbalanced energies
And I draw the best to me.
So mote it be."

While you're doing this spell, "fold" your wish or desire into your thoughts and feelings. Enjoy the scents of the essential oils and notice them lifting your emotions. Gaze at the soft, glowing candlelight and imagine it brightening your life. Envision positive, joyful vibrations flowing toward you and into you. Remain in the circle for as long as you like. When you're ready, extinguish the candles in the reverse order of how you lit them, to open the circle. Dab a little of your preferred oil on a cloth hanky and carry it with you during the day to sniff whenever you need a lift.

SIGNS OF THE TIMES

Long ago, Celtic prognosticators known as frithirs read signs of the times according to the first thing that caught their attention when they stepped outside. Try this ancient divination technique when you need guidance.

INGREDIENTS/TOOLS:
• None

- The first Monday after a solstice or equinox

Immediately after arising in the morning—before you do anything else—sit quietly for a few minutes and contemplate whatever you want advice about. Then go to your door and close your eyes. Take three slow, deep breaths then open the door and step outside (if you can do this safely with your eyes closed). Otherwise just stand in the open doorway facing out. Open your eyes. What's the first thing you see? What significance does it hold for you? A squirrel could suggest that you get busy gathering money, information, or other resources so you'll be prepared in difficult times ahead. A butterfly might mean a change for the better is coming or that you must transform the way you've been doing things in order to succeed.

Notice any impressions or feelings that arise into your awareness—they may be significant. If you don't sense an immediate answer, simply tuck away the memory of what you've seen and allow it to percolate in your subconscious. You might want to do some research into classic symbolism associated with the object that caught your attention. (My book *The Secret Power of Spirit Animals* gives lots of information about the meanings of animals and other creatures.) Pretty soon, perhaps in a dream, you'll receive the guidance you've been seeking.

HANG IN THERE SPELL

We all get discouraged at times. Instead of giving up, do this spell—it helps you hang in there until the situation improves.

INGREDIENTS**/T**OOLS**:**
- Oak flower essence (available in health food stores or online)
- 1 piece of yellow paper
- 1 pen or marker that writes red ink
- 1 black candle
- 1 candleholder
- Matches or a lighter
- 1 tarot card that represents you

- The tarot card Strength (which signifies inner and outer strength)
- The seven of wands tarot card (which represents the ability to hold firm when you're challenged or attacked)
- The Star tarot card (which symbolizes hope)
- The World tarot card (which indicates everything working out successfully)

BEST TIME TO PERFORM THE SPELL:
- As needed

Put a few drops of oak flower essence under your tongue; if you prefer, you can put the flower essence in a glass of water and drink it. On the paper, draw a red pentagram at least 1' in diameter. Lay it face up on your altar, a table, or another flat surface where it can remain for a time. Fit the candle in its holder, set it in the center of the pentagram, and light the candle.

Place the tarot card that represents you on the top point of the pentagram. Position the cards Strength and the seven of wands on the two side points of the pentagram. Put the Star and the World cards on the pentagram's bottom two points. Gaze at the cards and allow their symbolism to imprint your subconscious with positive imagery. Feel them stimulating the courage and confidence you need to face the challenges before you. Don't focus on your problems, just let your mind relax for a time. When you feel ready or start to lose your focus, extinguish the candle. Repeat as necessary, to reinforce your determination.

Chapter 18

TAKING THE NEXT STEP

If you've made it this far, congratulations. You've learned how to craft and cast all sorts of spells for all sorts of reasons. You've concocted potions and lotions, fashioned talismans and amulets, and mastered a variety of magick tools. Best of all, you've trained your mind and discovered your innate power to create effects in the manifest world. So where do you go from here?

KNOWLEDGE IS POWER

The world of magick is vast, maybe infinite. No matter how much you learn, there's always something else to explore just around the corner. One of the most respected astrologers of the twentieth century, Marc Edmund Jones, once said that he'd studied astrology for fifty years and barely scratched the surface. The same holds true for magick. Perhaps you've found a path that resonates with you. Or maybe you're still searching. Either way, you might wish to familiarize yourself with different schools of magick, even if you don't end up embracing them. Each can offer you something special, something you may not have known about before.

You may also like to delve deeper into fields such as astrology, numerology, feng shui, or tarot. These ancient arts will not only enhance your spellwork, they can open doors into fascinating realms and expand your understanding of yourself as well as the world around you.

Read as much as you can. You'll find a zillion books and online sites devoted to magickal practice and spellwork. Some focus on a particular area of interest, such as candle spells or goddess worship. Others provide a more comprehensive body of information. Each author and each teacher will likely approach things a bit differently, depending on his or her personal preferences and experiences. That's a good thing, because you don't want to limit yourself to only one perspective. Some you'll agree with, some you won't. Some you might decide to put aside for the time being and revisit later. That's okay, too.

Knowledge is power, as the saying goes. The more knowledge you have, the more powerful you'll become as a spellworker.

PRACTICE, PRACTICE, PRACTICE

Athletes and musicians know that in order to develop their talents they must practice. Spellcasters, too, must practice if they want to hone their craft and fulfill their potential. As I've said before, magick isn't a spectator sport. It's not for couch potatoes or the faint of heart. The more spells you do, the more comfortable you'll feel with the process and the more confident you'll become in your own ability. Try the following suggestions to sharpen your skills:

- Meditate regularly. Even ten minutes a day will help to focus your mind and ease stress.
- Practice sensing energy in plants, stones, places, people, etc. Everything in the world is composed of energy, so the more you can attune yourself to the energy patterns around you, the better you'll get at manipulating them with spells.

- Do spells often. Not only will frequent spellcasting help you to improve your life, it will make you more aware of how your thoughts, words, and deeds produce results.
- Try different types of spells.
- Practice working with various spell components: herbs, candles, crystals, etc.
- Pay attention to your dreams. As you delve into other levels of reality and expand your intuition, you may start having more vivid dreams and receive information in dream states. These insights can offer guidance in your waking life and in your magick practice.
- Keep a journal. We've already talked about the value of recording your spells and rituals in a book of shadows, but you may also want to keep a separate journal of your personal growth—because as you develop as a magician, your thinking and lots of other things may start to change as well. If you choose to include all this information in your book of shadows, that's fine, too.

MAKE FRIENDS WITH NATURE

Many of us spend so much time in climate-controlled offices, apartments, and automobiles that we've lost touch with the natural world. Kids play online games instead of softball. We text while walking instead of noticing the scenery around us.

Developing a rapport with the natural world can strengthen your skills as a spellworker, in part because many of the spell components you'll be using come from nature: herbs and flowers, gemstones and crystals. Additionally, you'll become more aware of your connection to the greater whole. You'll attune yourself to the cycles of earth and the heavens, so that you can work with them to empower your spells. You may even attract attention from the other creatures who share this planet with you and gain their help. How can you begin to tap nature's wisdom?

- Go for a walk without your cell phone or your tunes.
- Visit different places in nature—the woods, the waterfront, a hilltop—and experience the different energies in each of these places.
- Go outside at night and look at the sky for a while. Pretty awesome, huh?
- Pay attention to the moon's changing phases and their effects.
- Sit under a tree and try to sense it communicating with you.
- Sit beside a lake, stream, or other body of water and let it calm your mind.
- Hold different types of stones and see if you notice different resonances emanating from them.
- Watch birds, insects, and wildlife.
- Collect fallen leaves in autumn or press wildflowers in your book of shadows in the spring.
- Plant some seeds and watch them grow.

You might also like to welcome the sun each morning with a yoga practice known as the Sun Salutation. Or take a few minutes at dawn, noon, dusk, and midnight to sense the energy patterns around you. Even if you live in a high-rise in Manhattan, you can still walk in a park, grow plants in a container on a fire escape, and observe the changing seasons.

CREATING SPELLS FROM SCRATCH

After a while, you'll probably want to design some original spells. That's great. Following these steps will help you to create spells that can be just as effective as the ones you learn from this book and from other sources:

1. Boil down the purpose of the spell to a word or short phrase.
2. Find the ingredients suited to your goal.
3. Determine the best time to cast the spell.
4. Decide if you want to include an affirmation or incantation. If so, write one according to the instructions in Chapter 5.
5. Cleanse and purify all the objects you'll use in your spell.
6. Consider the order in which you'll do what you do.

7. Write your spell in your book of shadows, along with your experiences and outcome.

What kind of results can you expect from your spellwork? Well, that depends on you. Like a computer, spells do exactly what you tell them to do. So if you perform a spell to find a perfect companion and end up with a wonderful dog, your magick certainly has worked!

CRAFT IT YOURSELF

Want to kick your spells up a notch? Try crafting your own ingredients. When you do it yourself, you imbue the components of your spells with your personal energy and intention. From the very beginning, you empower these components to work with you to accomplish your goals. They become embodiments of your will. You might want to:

- Grow your own botanicals from seed. Start with a few hardy herbs, such as mint for prosperity spells, basil for protection, sage for purification, and marjoram for love and happiness. Gradually increase your magickal garden according to your needs and physical environment.
- Make your own candles. One of the easiest ways to do this is to purchase beeswax sheets and roll them into candles. You can also melt wax and pour it into molds, adding specially chosen essential oils and flower petals or leaves from your homegrown plants. Opt for soy wax rather than paraffin (which contains petroleum products), and use cotton wicks that don't have lead in them.
- Make your own loose incense. You can use any combination of resins and plant matter, so long as you're certain they're safe to inhale when burned. You will need: 1 part resin (combined or single resins) and 1 part dried plant matter. Grind the resin in a mortar and pestle or a coffee grinder, and then grind the plant material. Put the mix in a small bottle or jar, shake to combine, then cap and label your fragrant blend.
- Make your own herbal oils for anointing candles, gemstones, and talismans. Place a handful of your chosen plant material in a small saucepan, and pour a cup of light olive or safflower oil over it. Heat

the oil and plant matter gently over a low temperature for fifteen minutes, then pour the mixture into a clean jar. Cover the jar with a double layer of cheesecloth and fasten with a rubber band. Allow the oil to sit for ten days to two weeks, then strain it into a clean bottle; cap and label.

- Fashion seasonal wreaths and decorative arrangements from plants you've grown yourself, cuttings from favorite trees and shrubs, cones from evergreens, feathers you've found, and/or other natural materials.

You might also enjoy sewing pouches for amulets and talismans, sachets, and dream pillows, then stuffing them with botanicals from your garden. Learn to make your own paper for writing spells and affirmations—you can even add magick herbs or flowers to the mix. Craft ritual jewelry with gemstones and crystals. Have fun, but remember that each step of the process is an important part of your spellworking.

DOING MAGICK WITH OTHER PEOPLE

If you've been practicing solo, at some time you may consider spellworking with other like-minded people. If you already know someone you'd like to work with, great. If not, you might start checking around to see if a group of metaphysically oriented people already exists in your area. Yoga centers, health food cooperatives, and New Age stores can be good places to start.

Performing spells and rituals with other people can have advantages and disadvantages. Consider the plusses and minuses before you make any major commitments. On the plus side, for example:

- It can be fun to share ideas and spend time with "kindred spirits."
- You can learn a lot from other people's experiences.
- Combining your energy with someone else's can ramp up the power of a spell.

On the other hand:

- If your energies or intentions aren't compatible with those of the others in a group, your spells could get confused, diffused, or go totally awry.
- If you're working with people who tend to be domineering, or you're insecure about your own abilities, you might allow someone else to influence you unduly.

Being part of a group requires cooperation, respect, and tolerance, so choose your magickal companions carefully. They needn't be your close friends, but you should have some common ground and similar ideas about magick. Honesty, trust, and supportiveness between you are important. Make sure their ethics are compatible with yours. Establish boundaries and set guidelines for the rituals and spells you'll perform. Decide how you'll delegate responsibilities and iron out problems. Don't let anyone coerce you into doing anything that goes against your personal code. If something doesn't feel right, trust your instincts and bow out if necessary.

Perhaps you'd like to study with a teacher. Again, check out potential teachers carefully before you sign on with one:

- Find out as much as you can about his or her background.
- Discuss his or her expectations of you.
- Are you on the same wavelength spiritually?
- Do you hold similar magickal goals?
- Do you feel the teacher respects you and your opinions, instead of judging or trying to dominate you?
- Are the pace, schedule, and workload comfortable for you?
- If the teacher charges fees, are you comfortable with the amount and the reasons for the fees?

You might want to interview other spellcasters for recommendations. You can do some online research to find someone in your area who might be right for you to study with. Or you can do a spell to attract the perfect teacher. Remember the old saying "When the student is ready, the teacher will appear."

Between the time you began this book and now, you've come a long way. I hope that you feel the journey has been worthwhile, and that you've learned things you can build upon as you continue your work as a magician. Once you've started on this path, your life will never be the same. Magick transforms you. Your worldview changes, and as a consequence your interactions with everyone and everything you encounter in your daily life change, too. As Dr. Wayne Dyer often says, "When you change the way you look at things, the things you look at change."

In the process, you change the world. Remember that old saying about how a butterfly flapping its wings on one side of the globe influences the winds at the opposite side? It's true. Your energy, your thoughts, your actions impact everything else in the universe. And now that you possess a greater understanding of how this happens, you realize that you have the power to consciously create circumstances. That's an awesome responsibility and one you shouldn't take lightly. Every moment of every day, you have the ability to manifest the reality you desire, in yourself and the world around you—and every moment you'll be challenged to make choices about how you use that ability. The future resides with you. Embrace it!

APPENDIX: U·S·/METRIC CONVERSION CHARTS

VOLUME CONVERSIONS

U.S. Volume Measure	Metric Equivalent
⅛ teaspoon	0.5 milliliter
¼ teaspoon	1 milliliter
½ teaspoon	2 milliliters
1 teaspoon	5 milliliters
½ tablespoon	7 milliliters
1 tablespoon (3 teaspoons)	15 milliliters
2 tablespoons (1 fluid ounce)	30 milliliters
¼ cup (4 tablespoons)	60 milliliters
⅓ cup	90 milliliters
½ cup (4 fluid ounces)	125 milliliters
⅔ cup	160 milliliters
¾ cup (6 fluid ounces)	180 milliliters
1 cup (16 tablespoons)	250 milliliters
1 pint (2 cups)	500 milliliters
1 quart (4 cups)	1 liter (about)

WEIGHT CONVERSIONS

U.S. Weight Measure	Metric Equivalent
½ ounce	15 grams
1 ounce	30 grams
2 ounces	60 grams
3 ounces	85 grams
¼ pound (4 ounces)	115 grams
½ pound (8 ounces)	225 grams
¾ pound (12 ounces)	340 grams
1 pound (16 ounces)	454 grams

INDEX

The Modern Witchcraft Spell Book

The Modern Witchcraft Spell Book

Soup
  healing chicken and veggie,
    203–4
  Mabon, 260–61
  summer solstice gazpacho, 256
Spearmint, 135
Spell bottles, 82
Spellcasting
  benefits of, 18–19
  circle, 229–30
  vs. spellcrafting, 20
  steps to successful, 114, 134,
    152, 172, 188, 206, 226, 246,
    264
Spellcrafting, vs. spellcasting, 20
Spells. *See also specific spells*
  affirmations in, 66
  collecting ingredients for, 230
  composing, 23
  crafting ingredients for, 283–84
  creating, 282–83
  defined, 10, 16–17
  everyday, 16
  health and healing, 89, 187–204
  ingredients for, 23
  love, 88, 113–31
  miscellaneous, 263–78
  money and abundance, 89,
    133–40
  with others, 225–40
  purpose of, 10
  religion and, 17
  vs. rituals, 21–22
  safety and protection, 89,
    151–69
  seasonal, 241–61

self-improvement, 205–23
  success, 171–85
  timing of, 97–109
  use of, 17–18, 20–21
  using gemstones and crystals
    in, 57–59
  workings of, 19
Spellwork
  with angels, 93–94
  art of, 15–24
  preparing stones for, 56–57
  space for, 23, 37–47
  steps to successful, 22–24
  tradition of, 15–16
Spices, 116, 135, 153, 173, 189,
  208
Spicy sachet for protection, 158
Spirit animals, 90–92, 155–56,
  236–38
Spirits
  to help with spells, 215–16
  presence of, 38
  spell to banish, 157–58
  spell to call, 234–36
  spellwork with, 24, 87–96
Spring equinox, 107
Springtime smoothie, 254
Squash, 245
Star sapphire, 173
Stones, 55–59, 116, 135, 153, 173,
  189, 208
Strawberry, 244
Strength, 89
Strength and safety soup, 165–66
Stress-relieving spell, 272–73
Success spells, 171–85

The Modern Witchcraft Spell Book

ABOUT THE AUTHOR

Skye Alexander is the award-winning author of more than thirty fiction and nonfiction books, including *The Modern Guide to Witchcraft, The Everything® Wicca & Witchcraft Book, The Everything® Spells & Charms Book, Nice Spells/Naughty Spells, Good Spells for Bad Days,* and *The Everything® Tarot Book.* Her stories have been published in anthologies internationally, and her work has been translated into more than a dozen languages. The Discovery Channel featured her in the TV special *Secret Stonehenge* doing a ritual at Stonehenge. She divides her time between Texas and Massachusetts.